"You listen to her heartache, you care, y[ ] to do next. This clear, step-by-step book [ ] deal with painful realities. It doesn't promise any unrealistic quick fixes but instead lays out the path to the freedom of walking in God's ways."

— PAMELA REEVE, professor;
author of *Faith Is . . .* and *Parables of the Vineyard*

"You are holding a treasure chest full of wisdom, direction, and biblical insight. Cook and Volkhardt have carefully crafted an invaluable guide for every woman who has ever desired to see God bring hope and healing to others. As you turn these pages, be prepared to draw near to the true wonderful Counselor and watch Him transform your heart as well."

— ROBIN JONES GUNN, author of the SISTERCHICKS novels and the CHRISTY MILLER series

"*Kitchen Table Counseling* provides essential principles and tools in a simple readable format. Readers will find themselves empowered to incorporate and utilize these biblical guidelines in their daily lives."

— JOSEPH C. ALDRICH, president emeritus,
Multnomah Bible College and Seminary;
author of *Lifestyle Evangelism*

"All believers subscribe to God's ability to transform lives, but many of us are awkward when called upon to convey to struggling souls the truth we ardently believe. With advice seasoned by years of biblically based ministry, Muriel Cook and her daughter have given us a trustworthy guide that belongs on the ready-reference shelf of every person who desires to help others."

— JEANNE HENDRICKS, speaker; author of *A Mother's Legacy*

To my daughters, Shelly and Milei, whose lives and ministries I deeply respect. And to my spiritual daughters serving Christ around the world who are Kitchen Table Counselors.

—MURIEL

For Milei, my sister, my friend. I treasure you.

—SHELLY

kitchen table counseling

A PRACTICAL AND BIBLICAL GUIDE FOR WOMEN HELPING OTHERS

muriel l. cook and shelly cook volkhardt

NAVPRESS®

OUR GUARANTEE TO YOU

We believe so strongly in the message of our books that we are making this quality guarantee to you. If for any reason you are disappointed with the content of this book, return the title page to us with your name and address and we will refund to you the list price of the book. To help us serve you better, please briefly describe why you were disappointed. Mail your refund request to: NavPress, P.O. Box 35002, Colorado Springs, CO 80935.

The Navigators is an international Christian organization. Our mission is to advance the gospel of Jesus and His kingdom into the nations through spiritual generations of laborers living and discipling among the lost. We see a vital movement of the gospel, fueled by prevailing prayer, flowing freely through relational networks and out into the nations where workers for the kingdom are next door to everywhere.

NavPress is the publishing ministry of The Navigators. The mission of NavPress is to reach, disciple, and equip people to know Christ and make Him known by publishing life-related materials that are biblically rooted and culturally relevant. Our vision is to stimulate spiritual transformation through every product we publish.

ISBN 1-57683-795-5

Cover design by Brand Navigation, LLC—DeAnna Pierce, Bill Chiaravalle, www.brandnavigation.com
Cover photo by Stephen Gardner, Pixelworks Studio, www.shootpw.com
Creative Team: Rachelle Gardner, Arvid Wallen, Liz Heaney, Amy Spencer, Cara Iverson, Pat Reinheimer

Some of the anecdotal illustrations in this book are true to life and are included with the permission of the persons involved. All other illustrations are composites of real situations, and any resemblance to an individual living or dead is coincidental.

Unless otherwise identified, all Scripture quotations in this publication are taken from the *New American Standard Bible* (NASB), © The Lockman Foundation 1960, 1962, 1963, 1968, 1971, 1972, 1973, 1975, 1977, 1995. Other versions quoted include the HOLY BIBLE: NEW INTERNATIONAL VERSION® (NIV®). Copyright © 1973, 1978, 1984 by International Bible Society, used by permission of Zondervan Publishing House, all rights reserved; the *Amplified New Testament* (AMP), © The Lockman Foundation 1954, 1958; the *Holy Bible, New Living Translation* (NLT), copyright © 1996. Used by permission of Tyndale House Publishers, Inc., Wheaton, Illinois 60189. All rights reserved; and the *King James Version* (KJV).

Cook, Muriel L.
  Kitchen table counseling : a practical and biblical guide for women helping others / Muriel Cook and Shelly Cook Volkhardt.
    p. cm.
  Includes bibliographical references and index.
  ISBN 1-57683-795-5
  1. Women--Pastoral counseling of. 2. Women in church work.
  I. Volkhardt, Shelly Cook. II. Title.
  BV4445.C66 2006
  253'.082--dc22
                          2005018768

Printed in the United States of America

4 5 6 / 10 09 08 07

FOR A FREE CATALOG OF NAVPRESS BOOKS & BIBLE STUDIES,
CALL 1-800-366-7788 (USA) OR 1-800-839-4769 (CANADA)

contents

introduction

by Shelly Cook Volkhardt

My mom, Muriel Cook, is the most amazing woman I know. I can see her in my mind's eye, standing at the end of our street, rice paddies on either side, when she and Daddy were missionaries in Taiwan. Every week she met her Chinese coworker for an afternoon of visiting neighbors. They knocked on every door within walking distance of our home, sharing Christ with whoever would invite them in. Mom taught etiquette to Taiwanese beauty contestants at a local charm school, hosted countless guests, and led Bible studies. My sister, Milei, and I watched her dress for teas with Madame Chiang Kai-Shek, wife of the president, and prepare for events where she and Daddy would lift up the name of Jesus in English and Chinese.

Over and over again I saw Mom rise to the occasion, whether it was roller-skating in a crowd of Chinese partygoers, killing a large, poisonous snake outside our gate, or kneeling in prayer beside her bed. Stamped in my memory are the evenings when my parents sat with the light behind their backs and a hymnbook in their hands, singing my sister and me to sleep. I can still hear Mom harmonizing with my father as they taught us the great doctrines of the church without our even knowing it. She sat vigil over Daddy when he was unconscious and hung between life and death due to Japanese encephalitis B. I saw her trust God during those days and even testify of His goodness to the people who streamed in to comfort her.

Mom has faced enormous trials and challenges and learned *who* God is. Little did I realize that the principles she was teaching us by her words and example would have such an impact on others.

Even though Mom is not a professional counselor, her days continue to be filled with counseling. Students and women from around the world seek the God-given wisdom she has to share as Counselor-at-Large at Multnomah Bible College (she always makes it clear that her title is *not* to be confused with Large Counselor). I have heard more than one person tell her, "Muriel, I've been seeing a psychologist, and you have helped me more in one hour than he has in years!"

If you were to meet my mother, you would see a beautiful, mature woman. She is a classy dresser, a bright spirit, crazy-in-love with my dad, and profoundly biased about her two daughters. Her gentle and approachable style, combined with her unwavering faith in our beloved Savior and the healing power of truly knowing Him, make others hungry to know Him too.

Many women in her life want to be just like her. That has been my goal too. One of the greatest compliments a person can pay me is to say, "You are just like your mother." Of course, it's only partially true; I am my own person. However, as I have put her material into written form, I have been surprised that most of the principles I thought were my own are actually what Mom taught me. She is so gifted in sharing truth that she makes you feel as if it was your idea in the first place!

A skilled communicator and popular speaker, Mom has committed her life to training, encouraging, and discipling women. Because her time and energy are limited, the best way to share her with you is with this book.

We have written it for women who love God and have found themselves listening to the problems of other women across the kitchen table, over the phone, standing in line at the store, and elsewhere. If you have wondered, *How can I help somebody with her problems?* this book is for you.

Kitchen Table Counseling is divided into two parts. Part 1 will help you understand the qualifications of a Kitchen Table Counselor (KTC) and give you an overview of your responsibilities and role as a KTC. It will show you how you can transition from crisis counseling to more of a discipling relationship and will offer advice for keeping your KTC ministry in balance.

In part 2 we'll show you how to take the principles you learn in part 1 and apply them to your counseling. Through stories and examples from actual counseling sessions, you will find help for knowing what to ask, what Scripture to use, and how you can help your counselee grow and develop. (The dialogues quoted in this book are similar to actual interactions between my mom and counselees; though not word for word, they have been created to give you an idea of what was said and of what you might say in your own counseling sessions.)

At the end of the book we've also included some information for leaders about how to use *Kitchen Table Counseling* to teach other women to become KTCs. You'll also find a list of Scriptures that offer insight into how to address many of the problems women face.

It is a sacred honor for me as a daughter, disciple, and active KTC myself who has been in this ministry for most of my life, to preserve in print the wisdom and insight God has given my mom. We do not intend for this material to be exhaustive. We are simply sharing with you the principles God has taught us that have been helpful in our lives and in the lives of others.

As you read this book, we pray that you will seek His face for the people who come across your path and that you will grow in confidence that God is all you need.

PART 1:

guidelines for the kitchen table counselor

"i need help! can i talk with you?"

Since I was twelve years old people have been telling me their problems and deepest secrets. I've spent thousands of hours listening to others talk about their hurts. Sometimes the people who talk to me are strangers. Once a filling station attendant (in Oregon we still have those) told me about his divorce while he was pumping gas into my car. A housekeeper at a motel where I was staying poured out her life story when she brought me an extra towel.

Another stranger addressed me not long ago when I was in the produce section of a grocery store. She looked at me from the other side of the sweet potato bin and announced, "I'm mad!"

"Why are you mad?" I asked.

"I'm furious with my husband," she replied and proceeded to tell me the story of her disintegrating marriage.

Most of the time, though, the women who talk to me know me. They may be a friend, a relative, a neighbor, a coworker, a student at the college where I work as a lay counselor, or someone who has heard me speak.

That was the case with Helen. She came to see me on the

recommendation of a friend of hers. She told me that it had been five years since her daughter's murder, but she was still searching for peace. She said, "I've gone to ministers, psychiatrists, everybody. Nobody can tell me how to get healed. I asked the last minister I counseled with if he thought I had to forgive the murderer for killing my daughter. He told me, 'You can't. Only God can do the forgiving.' But that didn't help me!"

When I heard her story, I told Helen, "You can't forgive your daughter's murderer, but Christ in you can. You do not forgive the murderer because he deserves your forgiveness, but because Jesus asks you to forgive him. The last sentence of Matthew 18:35 says to forgive others 'from your heart.' The only way you can do that is if you remember the promise, 'I can do all things through Him who strengthens me'" (Philippians 4:13). Then I took Helen through some simple steps to forgiveness (see chapter 4). Together we got on our knees and laid her burden at Jesus' feet. Afterward she said to me, "I am free! For the first time in five years I have peace."

LEARNING GOD'S REMEDIES

I couldn't have handled a situation as serious as Helen's when women first started talking to me about their hurts and problems. There were times as a pastor's wife and even as a missionary when I felt as though I was near breaking under the heaviness of the unspeakable things people told me in confidence. Physically, emotionally, and spiritually I was unable to carry these burdens and still fulfill my role as wife, mother, and Christian. But while our family was still living in Taiwan, I began to see that these women did not need my advice, nor was I capable of providing what they longed for. What they needed was *God's answers to their heart cries.*

I knew that someday I would have to stand before God and answer for what I encouraged other women to do. So I began to seek His remedies for people's burdens. I knew that if I was to help those who came to me, I needed to be able to apply God's Word to their situations. The

Bible has concrete answers and fundamental principles for how we are to live. God's Word is living and active (see Hebrews 4:12). It gives us all we need for life and godliness, and through the Holy Spirit we have access to God's divine power (see 2 Peter 1:3).

As I read and studied the Bible, I prayed and asked God to show me His principles for living. If I needed His counsel for a particular problem that a woman had brought to me, I would start right where I had been reading in my Bible and ask Him to speak to me. I underlined the verses whenever I came on a truth that applied to an issue that would help someone I was working with. Then in the margin I wrote the topic it addressed. This allowed me to find the verses easily because, even though I have always found it difficult to remember specific references, I can remember the vicinity of a verse.

In time, I came to call this God-given ministry to women "kitchen table counseling." That phrase gives a picture of what I do. Although I am not a professional counselor, I reach out to hurting women sitting across my kitchen table, using scriptural truth and spiritual encouragement.

TRAINING OTHERS IN
KITCHEN TABLE COUNSELING

I began to teach other women how to become Kitchen Table Counselors (KTCs) when we moved back to the United States after sixteen years in Asia. Our family settled into a neighborhood church near our mission headquarters in California. The pastor was a wonderful, gentle man whom we grew to love. We were shocked to learn that he had become sexually involved with a woman he had been counseling. His fall into immorality devastated and bewildered the congregation.

The church called a new pastor, who realized the dangers of pastors counseling needy women. He knew about my ministry of Kitchen Table Counseling and asked me to help train a group of women to aid him.

He wanted to be able to call on these women as a resource when other women in the church needed counseling or someone to come alongside them during a difficult period.

Some of the would-be KTCs had natural gifts for counseling and an ability to relate well to people. Others were wise, with many years of church experience. A few were young in the Lord. Each woman had a variety of gifts and abilities, a heart to know God, and a hunger to seek His solutions for her own challenges as well as those of others. I taught these women the principles God had shown me, and Kitchen Table Counseling seminars were born. That was thirty-six years ago.

My role as a KTC became official when my husband, Norm, and I started working at Multnomah Bible College in Portland, Oregon. The school asked me to counsel and encourage female students as well as wives of the seminary and graduate students. They gave me an office, and although I no longer have a kitchen table, I have created a comfortable, home-like environment where women can feel safe to share their hearts.

Over the years I have been asked to train groups of women in many churches. Almost everyone—from the director of women's ministry to the small-group leader to the quiet woman in the pew—feels the need to be better equipped to help others. In the Fall 1994 Lectureship at Multnomah Bible College, counselor Dan Allender spoke to the students on the theme of "The Bible and Psychology." He told them that spiritual counseling needs to be done by people in the church and that people shrink from dealing with spiritual issues on a spiritual level. I agree, and that's one reason I'm writing this book.

What I've written comes out of my own experience as I've depended on God to help me deal with the problems women face on a spiritual level. I believe that God can help you do the same, regardless of your gifts and abilities. So keep reading!

"am i really qualified to be a ktc?"

I answered the phone and could hear the distinctive crackle of an overseas call. Rebecca, a young woman I had met at Multnomah Bible College, was on the other end of the line. She and her husband had moved to South America, and as she became more proficient in Spanish, women began to come to her about their concerns. Rebecca told me, "I am working with a woman who was abused as a child. I have never dealt with anything like this. All I can do is pray for her; I don't know how to help her. What would *you* say to her? What can I do?" Before answering her question, I assured Rebecca that God had clearly put that woman in her life and that He wanted her to be a KTC, His channel of healing and encouragement.

If you are wondering if you would be able to counsel other women, know that everyone questions her ability to help others, particularly in extreme circumstances. I too used to worry that I wouldn't know how to help someone, that I wouldn't know what to say or do. Now I know that such feelings of inadequacy are natural and normal.

Let's take a look at some common fears women have about being a KTC, along with my responses.

COMMON FEARS

What if I'm not a professional counselor and have never had any training? Can I still help women with deep hurts and problems?

Because you are reading this book, it's likely you have a heart for women and want to know how you can help them. When it comes to being a KTC, these qualities are far more valuable than a professional degree in counseling. You could have all the education in the world, but if you don't have a heart for helping people, your efforts will not have any impact.

In ourselves, we are *not* capable, but God can make us adequate. He can give us what we need to help those He puts in our path. If you are His child, God has given you gifts, gifts that He wants you to use for His purposes. The apostle Paul wrote, "For to one is given the word of wisdom through the Spirit, and to another the word of knowledge according to the same Spirit; to another faith by the same Spirit" (1 Corinthians 12:8-9). It is possible that God has gifted you with wisdom, knowledge, mercy, faith, or a combination of these characteristics.

Don't be afraid that you won't have anything to offer women who are more educated than you or have more skills than you. You can encourage them by telling how God has worked in your life—how you mothered, how you made it in your marriage, how He brought you through crises, and how you juggled work and having children.

What if I don't have any experience with a particular problem? Can I really be a help to that person?

In a word, yes. A KTC doesn't need to have a personal experience with a problem in order to help someone with that problem. Jesus never intended for us to experience all the agonies of sin, which can leave us scarred. He wants us to learn wisdom through discernment. When He lived on the earth, He was not experienced in sin, yet He had compassion and understanding for sinners. He can give you His heart and His wisdom. He can give you all you need to help someone.

Because I work on a college campus, I often counsel women who have been promiscuous or have been raped or molested. Many times, at the end of our time together, I ask if they know whether I've been raped, molested, or promiscuous. Invariably, they respond, "No, I don't know whether you were or not."

Then I ask, "Did it matter? Was I able to help you in the Lord?" I've never had a counselee say that my lack of personal experience got in the way of my being able to help.

Neither do we need to tell people the details of our own experiences in order to help them. In fact, if we share specifics, it can put sordid details in the front of their minds when they think about us. This causes the focus to shift to what happened to us and away from Jesus. It's not that God can't use our past; He can. But we must be very sure that the Holy Spirit wants us to use it and that He shows us how.

Our identity should not be in our sin — whatever it was — or in how we have been damaged. Our identity must be in Jesus. If your experience with sin comes to light in your counseling, put the emphasis on the fact that you are forgiven and that the Lord has restored you and brought you out.

I love God and want to serve Him, but I don't feel I know enough about His Word to use it to help others.

As long as you have an attitude that says, "I want for you to teach me more, Lord," a lack of Bible knowledge isn't a hindrance for the KTC. If you do not know God's Word, begin to study it now. Spend time alone with God, daily reading His Word. I think you will be surprised by how often your daily reading will address things you or your counselee are facing. Mark the passages in your Bible that refer to specific problems. You might also keep a list of references, divided by topics, in the back of your Bible (and see the Topical Scripture Reference Index at the end of this book, the list I use). When God shows you verses or passages on forgiveness, fear, suffering, His purposes, and so on, add them to your topic list on the blank pages in the back of your Bible. They can give you wisdom for what to say and do with women who come to you for help.

If a woman raises a question you can't answer, simply tell her, "I'll get back to you," and then search the Word for help on the subject. Pray and ask God for wisdom. Read respected authors (you'll find books recommended throughout *Kitchen Table Counseling*). Also, ask others for input and prayer support (without violating confidentiality), for "in abundance of counselors there is victory" (Proverbs 11:14).

We can share only what God has taught us. This principle is underlined in Deuteronomy, "Only give heed to yourself and keep your soul diligently, so that you do not forget the things which your eyes have seen and they do not depart from your heart all the days of your life; but make them known to your sons and your grandsons" (4:9).

Don't some problems require the help of a professional? How can I know when to send a counselee to one?

Yes, it is important to know when to send someone to a professional. Keep in mind that the source of many problems of the heart and soul can be a sick body. Send a woman to see a doctor for a thorough physical checkup if she comes to you with:

- depression
- a major sexual problem
- low energy levels
- rapid weight gain or loss
- unusual difficulty sleeping
- breathing problems
- an eating disorder

Send her to a professional counselor or therapist if she is struggling with any of the following:

- threats of suicide
- sexual abuse
- rape
- physical abuse
- an eating disorder
- self-destructive behaviors
- panic attacks (This refers to a sudden, mounting terror or panic that can come "out of the blue" or in response to experiencing or thinking about a situation. A visit to a medical doctor may also be helpful.)
- addictions
- self-mutilation
- pornography (use by spouse or self)

Keep a list of good, reputable Christian counselors in your area to whom you can refer women. If you need help compiling such a list, ask a Christian physician or get recommendations from people you respect. You might want to keep a list of counselors' addresses, phone numbers, areas of expertise, and fee schedules. (If you need further recommendations, Focus on the Family has a National Referral Network. You can call 719-531-3400 extension 7700 and ask for names of godly Christian counselors in your area.)

When you send a woman to see a professional counselor, *don't stop meeting with her.* A psychiatrist recently told me that apart from professional help, the greatest aid to a woman struggling with an emotional problem is someone who will pray with her, check up on her, and hold her accountable for the counseling she is receiving from her counselor or therapist. A KTC can come alongside a woman who is seeing a professional counselor by:

- monitoring her physical problems
- holding her accountable to follow through on medical and/or psychological appointments
- meeting with her to process her sessions and line up what she is learning with God's Word
- encouraging her to find ways to apply what she is learning
- believing God for her when she doubts
- praying with her and for her

Remember, God is not interested in how much we know, but in how much we have learned from what He has already shown us. So instead of looking at what you don't have, look at what you *do* have that might qualify you to be a KTC.

AN EFFECTIVE KTC . . .

Is Willing for God to Use Her

If you are willing, God can use you to touch everyone you are with. The heartfelt prayer of an effective KTC is "You open the door, Lord, and I'll go through it. You cause them to ask and I promise to be faithful to speak for You."

God wants us to be His mouthpiece, and He can help us be alert to opportunities to represent Him when we are with others. You can bring His light to the world's darkness by "always being ready to make a defense to everyone who asks you to give an account for the hope that is in you, yet with gentleness and reverence" (1 Peter 3:15).

Knows That God Will Give Her Wisdom

If you seek God's face, He will give you wisdom for helping others, for "in [Christ] are hidden all the treasures of wisdom and knowledge" (Colossians 2:3). A KTC's confidence comes from her dependence on the One who has all that she needs to know.

Proverbs 1:7 tells us that "the fear of the LORD is the beginning of knowledge." One way to understand the phrase "the fear of the LORD" is to replace it with "the recognition of God's power and His presence." So, the verse could read, "The recognition of God's power and His presence is the beginning of knowledge." In other words, we gain knowledge by learning to recognize God's power and presence in every aspect of our life.

As you tune your heart to His by cultivating a constant awareness of His perspective and power, He will give you insight into people and what they are dealing with. He will show you how to help them. As my counselees sit across from me, I pray with every breath, "Lord, give me wisdom." Often, after a counseling session, I am amazed at what God has given me. His Word and His wisdom can transform a person and her thinking.

Cultivates Her Walk with God and Spends Time in His Word

This is one of the most important qualities of a KTC. If you will seek to keep Jesus as your first love, He will change your heart. When He is your top priority, He has room to work His character into your life.

Oswald Chambers wrote, "Our Lord's first obedience was to the will of His Father, not to the needs of men. . . . If I am devoted to the cause of humanity only, I will soon be exhausted and come to the place where my love will falter; but if I love Jesus Christ personally and passionately, I can serve humanity though men treat me as a door-mat."[1] These words convict me. At times I have been so taken up with "my ministry" that it has become more important to me than my walk with God. When that happens, my strength is depleted and I find that I am angry with the very people I am trying to help. Sometimes I even get mad at God. I've found myself saying, "God, I give You myself, my time — and You're not blessing *my* ministry."

Whose ministry is it? When we focus on what we are doing and not on Him, our perspectives and priorities can become confused.

Seeks to Be Authentic

A college student once told me, "My father was a Christian, but he was miserable to live with. As a believer, he toed the line, but he was mean, stern, and grumpy. I tried to run away from God for ten years because I thought God was like him. Because of that, I didn't want to have anything to do with Jesus." Sad to say, the father's inconsistency caused his daughter and likely others to be on guard around him. This father was not authentic. Being authentic means being the same at home as we are at church or anywhere else in public.

One of the most authentic and captivating people I know is eighty-five years old. She is a retired missionary with a low income and physical limitations that make it difficult for her to walk. Yet she celebrates life. She loves God and others. She has her hair and nails done, dresses up every day, laughs and cries with others, and talks and shares about her own life. This woman has more invitations in a week than many people half her age have in a year.

One day I asked her what was her secret in life. She answered, "For the past forty years I have had hanging over my bed two plaques that are my mottoes. One says, 'Prayer Changes Things' and the other, 'Not Somehow but Triumphantly.'" The two spiritual principles that she kept always before her had filtered into every aspect of her life. Not only did she live out what she believed every day, but her authenticity attracted others to her.

Some people think that being real means "letting it all hang out," telling everything about your own life. But we can be authentic without telling others everything we feel and think and have done. Authenticity is more about being consistent in who you are than it is about what you say.

So ask yourself, "Are my actions and attitudes consistent with what I believe about Jesus?" If so, you are authentic. As you cultivate and keep your excitement about God, His work will be fresh in your heart — and you will be a delight to others.

Is Willing to Let God Change Her

We don't have to be perfect for God to use us to help others. But we do need to listen to Him and others and be open to allowing Him to make us more like Christ.

God can use any part of His creation to help us become more aware of areas in need of change. For instance, He used our last dog to show me more about relaxing. She would flatten herself out on the carpet with her legs stretched out as far as possible in both directions, put her head down, and rest. Her total abandon to relaxation caused me to realize that I needed to take time to do the same.

God often uses other people to help us become aware of parts of ourselves that need polishing. When I was in high school, several of my friends said that before they got to know me, they thought I was stuck up. I had no idea I had been sending out that message. It grieved me, because my greatest desire was to glorify God and serve Him. At first I dismissed the idea because it wasn't true; after all, I truly didn't feel that I was better than anybody else. However, it slowly became clear that the message I was giving to others was keeping some at arm's length, making it impossible for me to develop a good relationship with them. So I asked God to show me what others saw.

It wasn't long before He answered that prayer. One day I was reading the list in Proverbs 6:16-19 of seven things the Lord hates. One of those is a proud or haughty look, and the words leaped off the page and smacked me. I knew God was telling me that was my problem. I told Him, "Lord, something about my expression or the look in my eye is not revealing the intention of my heart. Help my face to be so open that it says to people, 'I like you, I care about you, I am interested in and approve of you.'"

It is hard to hear things that others don't like about us. I used to think that my ego was terribly fragile and that if I was doing my best and could do no more, more criticism would be too hard to take. But I was actually being self-protective. One day it dawned on me that I was behaving like an ostrich. When an ostrich puts his head in the sand, guess what part of his body sticks up for everyone to see? It's the ugliest thing about him! I realized that if I wasn't willing to hear difficult things about myself, then the ugliest part of me would stay right out in the forefront.

So pay attention to how people interact with you. Do they make little jokes or backhand references, such as, "Oh, she's always late," or "You know she's disorganized; she never calls back"? Take note. They could be pointing out one of your blind spots. If we listen and are willing to learn, God can help us deal with our unpolished sides. Yet the lovely thing about God is that He will use us right where we are—in the middle of our process!

WE ARE ALL IN PROCESS

As Kitchen Table Counselors we do not have to have our life together before God can use us to help others. But it's important that we tell those we meet with that we are in process: "I don't know everything—God is still teaching me, and it is possible that I will disappoint you in some respect" and then to remind them that only Jesus never disappoints: "AND HE WHO BELIEVES IN HIM WILL NOT BE DISAPPOINTED" (1 Peter 2:6).

Do you have the qualities of a KTC, or are you willing to cultivate those qualities? If so, you can minister to other women. God wants you to be yielded and available to Him. He will use your willing heart.

getting a handle on the big picture

The first time I met with Mary, she had recently come from an appointment with a psychiatrist. He was the third she'd gone to with her problem. Her husband, an intelligent, capable professor at a prominent university, was having an affair. The third psychiatrist's answer was the same as the other two she'd consulted: "Your self-image has taken a battering, and you need to boost it. Why don't you go and have an affair of your own?"

Mary had no religious background, but she was smart enough to know that an affair would only compound her difficulties. Was there anybody out there who could help her? In desperation she picked up the phone book, opened the Yellow Pages to "Churches," closed her eyes, and stabbed her finger randomly on the page. She dialed the number nearest the tip of her nail and asked for an appointment.

When Mary unloaded her burden in the pastor's office, he told her, "I'll be sending a woman to see you. She'll help you walk through this." When she left, he called me. If I had not been convinced of God's promise to guide me and of some key biblical principles, I would have run the other way.

Many of the women I've trained to become KTCs have concerns about what they are supposed to *do* in a counseling session. Initially, I did too. In this chapter I want to share with you the biblical principles that guide my approach to counseling. Keep in mind that because no two women are the same, there is no cookie-cutter approach to dealing with problems. However, these foundational principles will give you "the big picture" of your role and responsibilities as a KTC.

Keep in mind that all six of these principles may not apply to every counseling situation and that the order in which they apply to a particular counseling situation may be different from what is presented here. While I always seek God's guidance before and throughout a counseling relationship, these principles can be applied in any order, depending on the situation and how God leads.

Let's return to Mary's story so that I can show you how I applied these principles in my approach to helping her.

PRINCIPLE 1:

ASK FOR GOD'S GUIDANCE

In the car on the way to Mary's house, I wondered, *How can I help this woman?* The pastor had told me that she was an atheist. I knew I needed God's guidance because He knew what was in her heart while I did not. So I prayed, "Lord, what am I going to do? Prepare me, flow through me, forgive me of anything that I have in my heart that would keep You from speaking through me. Let me be a clean channel through which You can touch Mary. Help me know what to say to this woman; give me Your wisdom and let me use only Your words."

I know that my power as a KTC comes from God. As I daily walk with a consciousness of *who* He is and *what* He can do, I plug into the Power Source. Recognizing His presence and power helps me to look to Him for all that I need for living and for helping others. If I do not seek Him, I become simply an advice-giver, and I bear the responsibility for what happens in the lives of those I counsel. I rob them of God's perspective.

So before I met with Mary, I did what I always do before meeting with someone:

- I made sure my heart was right with God. I asked Him to show me anything that would hinder the free flow of His Spirit through me (see 2 Timothy 2:21).
- I invited Him to direct my heart, to attune my spirit to His direction for the needy one He had placed in my path (see 1 Corinthians 2:13).
- I prayed for wisdom and trusted Him to provide generously (see James 1:5).
- I asked Him to put a guard over my mouth so that I would only say what He would have me say (see Psalm 141:3).

After seeking God's guidance, I realized that before I could meet Mary's spiritual needs, I needed to encourage her to tell me her story.

PRINCIPLE 2:

LANCE THE BOIL

Because I know that God works when we acknowledge our hurts and wounds, the first thing I did with Mary was to ask her to tell me about her problem. She sobbed her heart out as she described her husband's betrayal. Mary needed to acknowledge, out loud, what had happened and how it had made her feel. I sensed that she wasn't ready for me to offer solutions. My goal for that first meeting was to get her to articulate what was going on in her life and the reason for the emotional state she was in. In this way, we opened up the "boil" that was causing her pain.

This principle is rooted in Romans 12:15, "Rejoice with those who rejoice, and weep with those who weep," and in Hebrews 13:3, "Remember those in prison *as if you* were their fellow prisoners, and those who are mistreated *as if you yourselves* were suffering" (NIV, emphasis mine). These passages remind KTCs that we need to always put ourselves in the counselee's shoes, emotionally and intellectually. We do this initially by having her tell us her story, no matter how humiliating it is.

LISTEN FOR MISCONCEPTIONS

Ask the Holy Spirit for discernment about what lies a counselee is believing that not only keep her from healing, but also continue to hurt her. Satan loves to keep us from the truth. I hear women make all kinds of untrue statements, such as, "I'm a bad person," "God must not love me," "I can't do anything right."
Many women have deep wounds. The Enemy takes advantage of that wounding and whispers lies into the wounded heart. Most people begin to believe and act on those lies.

A hurting or troubled person often has pockets of infection resulting from hurts that are deep in her soul. When the Scripture is applied at the appropriate time, it becomes the truth that heals. However, many biblical counselors try to give the medicine for the wound—answers from the Bible—*before* the wound has been cleaned out. This can inoculate or turn a person against God's Word. Even if we put the right medication (the Word of God) on a boil, it will not heal because it must be lanced so the infection can be released. When we acknowledge our pain and what causes it, that is equivalent to opening the boil and cleaning it out.

After hearing her story, I realized that Mary needed to forgive her husband. I've found this is often the bottom-line problem that needs to be addressed before deep healing can occur (see chapter 4). But I also realized that she was not ready to hear that she had forgiveness work to do. Before she could forgive her husband, Mary had to first give her heart to Jesus and experience His forgiveness. But she wasn't even ready to hear *that,* so for the first few months, I simply listened to Mary's hurts. I also met her felt need.

PRINCIPLE 3:
MEET HER FELT NEED

After our initial meeting, Mary began to call me three times a day, some-times more. Many times she was hysterical. One night she sobbed, "My husband is coming home for dinner and I can't manage to cook!" I knew that before I could ever share with Mary her need for a Savior, I had to help her get to a less desperate place. I needed to meet her felt need. This is what Jesus did with many of the hurting people who came to Him for help. He often addressed people's felt needs before He met their spiritual needs. Consider these examples:

- When Jairus asked Jesus to heal his daughter, Jesus went immediately, and addressed the belief issue later (see Mark 5:22-43; Luke 8:40-56).
- Jesus calmed the storm before He spoke to the disciples about their lack of faith (see Luke 8:22-25).
- Jesus allowed the sinful woman to weep, anoint His feet, and wipe them with her hair before He forgave her sins (see Luke 7:36-50).
- Jesus healed the crippled man at the pool of Bethesda before He ever spoke to him about sin (see John 5:1-15).

While I wanted to help Mary, I knew that it would not truly help her if I went to her house and fixed dinner for her. That would have made her dependent on me. Instead I needed to help get her over the hurdle that was keeping her from being able to cook dinner.

I asked her, "If you *could* cook, what would you cook?"

"Oh, I have a chicken," she replied.

"If you could fix it, what would you do? Fry, bake, or roast it?"

She answered, "I would fry it."

"I'll stay on the line. Get your chicken out of the refrigerator, put it on the counter, get your pan out—don't turn on the burner—then come back to the phone."

When Mary came back to the phone, I told her, "When I don't think I can fix dinner, I ask God to help me. Can I ask Him to help you?" Mary never refused my prayers on her behalf. Holding the phone, I prayed, "Lord, help Mary to know that You love her, that You are with her, and that You will help her cook dinner. In Jesus' name, amen." Once Mary got started cooking, the rest of the dinner came a bit more easily.

For four months, I prayed with Mary and coached her through the normal steps of life until she was able to cope with everyday living. I sought to help her deal with her pressing needs in order to guide her—someday—to Jesus.

PRINCIPLE 4:
TAKE HER TO JESUS

This and the remaining principles are taken from Mark 2:1-12. You know the story. Jesus was in Capernaum teaching. So many people wanted to hear Him that the home where was He staying was packed; there was no room for anyone else. Four men arrived at the house, carrying a paralyzed man on a cot, but they could not get through the crowd. Undeterred, they went onto the flat, earthen roof, typical of homes during Jesus' day, and began to dig a hole. When the opening was large enough, they carefully let down the cot and laid the man at Jesus' feet. He took one look at the paralytic, saw the faith of the four men, and said, "Son, your sins are forgiven" (verse 5). After some discussion with a few disapproving spiritual leaders, Jesus spoke again to the man, "I say to you, get up, pick up your pallet and go home" (verse 11). The Bible says the paralytic *immediately* got up and went home.

The paralytic's four friends knew where to look for hope and where to go for help. In the same way, my responsibility as a biblical counselor is to take to Jesus those who come across my path. I did this with Mary every time I met with her, including that first day. I can still recall our conversation.

Mary answered the doorbell, eyed me suspiciously, and didn't invite me in. I told her my name and said that the pastor had sent me. "Are you a professional counselor?" she asked.

"No, I'm not." (I never pretend to be something I'm not.)

"Are you a marriage counselor?" she asked.

I could have told her that I'd counseled hundreds of couples, but I said, "No, I'm not." Then she raised her voice, practically screaming in desperation, "Can you help me?"

"No, I can't," I replied. "But God can, if you'll let Him."

I want every woman I counsel to know who *can* help her. If Mary had told me, "I don't want your God; I don't believe in Him," then I would have said, "I have nothing else to give you. This is what I have and it works for me. I know it will work for you." But Mary opened the door and let me in. That first meeting I did nothing but take her to Jesus and hear her story, but she called me back for another appointment.

I constantly told Mary that God is the one who helps us and that I was there to simply offer His help to her. Even though Mary has a PhD and may have thought this sounded simplistic, I knew she was desperate for help and that God is the only one who has power for healing. When there was a period of calm, I would tell her, "Mary, do you know why you've come this far? Because Jesus loves you and He's been with you the whole time."

When Mary began to cope better with normal life, I invited her to my home for Bible study once a week. For two years she came, and I taught her about Jesus. One day she announced, "Today I'm ready."

"For what?" I asked.

"I am ready to give my heart to your God. Do you know what has kept me coming these past two years? That first day, when I asked you if you could help me, you said, 'No, but God can,' and you were so sure. Now I am sure too."

PRINCIPLE 5:

BELIEVE FOR HER

Almost everyone who comes to me in a crisis is running low on faith. Some are strong Christians, but their misery has drained their trust. Others don't believe in Jesus at all. I used to think, *I can't help a person if she doesn't believe in God or accept the authority of the Bible.* But Mark 2 helped me realize that this concern isn't valid. Jesus worked according to the faith of the men who carried their friend to Him. The Bible says nothing about the faith of the sick man, yet Jesus healed him *and* forgave his sins.

When I realized this, I began to wonder what God could do if He worked according to *my* faith. This challenge changed my outlook on Kitchen Table Counseling. It helped me understand that I can believe God for my counselee, even when she is struggling with her faith. Of course, she eventually has to choose to follow God for herself, but I can hold her up, pray with her, and keep her focused on God and His Word.

Mary needed me to believe God for her when she couldn't do it for herself. The God to whom we can carry everything is in the business of doing miracles: "With man this is impossible, but with God all things are possible" (Matthew 19:26, NIV). He is the God of the impossible.

I believed for Mary by putting her at Jesus' feet, because I know that He is the only one who can meet all our needs. I believed for her by praying *for* her and *with* her. Her ability to trust God was weak, but I knew Him and I knew that He was able to make a difference in her life. I took every opportunity to show Mary that by saying, "When I get into a situation like that, I talk to God about it. Would you let me do that with you right now?" I often prayed with Mary over the phone, and I made sure she knew I was praying for her at other times as well. I believed for her until she was able to believe for herself.

Believing for someone does not mean making unrealistic promises about what God might do. Contrary to what many Christians think, God doesn't promise us happiness. The Declaration of Independence gives U.S. citizens the "right" to the pursuit of happiness, but many Christians seem to equate that with a scriptural promise and often assume that everyone is entitled to be happy. That simply isn't biblical. I could not say to Mary, "God is going to put this marriage back together" or "God is not going to let this man leave you." I can't know all of God's purposes in my own life, let alone in others'. But I *can* be sure that God has a purpose for His children. I often told Mary, "Jesus *loves* you and He thinks you are lovely. He wants you to know Him."

God's plan is that we come to know Him and become like Christ. According to the apostle Paul, "We know that God causes all things to work together for good to those who love God, to those who are called according to His purpose . . . to become conformed to the image of His Son" (Romans 8:28-29). Most Kitchen Table Counseling consists of encouraging women to know Christ and helping them understand that He wants to use the events in their lives to change them to become more like Him.

When a woman comes to talk to me, I ask myself, *What could she be if she lived up to all the potential that God has placed in her?* I choose to see her from God's perspective. I ask God to help me look beyond her old scars, sin, and ugliness, and I believe God for the restoration of "the years the locusts have eaten" (Joel 2:25, NIV). In my heart I see the end result of what she will be, and I pray that she can see herself through my eyes and ultimately through God's. Part of fulfilling the scriptural call to "rejoice with those who rejoice" (Romans 12:15, NIV) is to be a cheerleader who strengthens and helps another to develop as *she* believes God for the work He wants to do in women's lives.

PRINCIPLE 6:
HELP HER BECOME INDEPENDENTLY DEPENDENT

The four men in Mark 2 carried the paralytic to Christ. Once they had lowered him to the feet of Jesus, their responsibility was to let the Lord take over. Jesus forgave the man of his sins and then told him to pick up his mat and walk. When he did what Jesus said, he demonstrated that he believed God for himself. He was now independently dependent on God.

This principle reflects the ultimate goal of the Kitchen Table Counselor. If those we work with become dependent on *us,* we do them more harm than help because we will not always be available to them. We must be careful that we don't fall into the trap of believing that we are indispensable to those we counsel. It is not healthy for us or the other people. We can trust God to be enough for them.

I constantly reminded Mary (and myself) that my goal was to make her independently dependent on God alone, and that when I was unavailable, she could talk to Him. My goal was to help her depend on Him, even if her circumstances didn't turn out the way we would have liked. If Mary's husband chose to leave, I wanted her to know that God would comfort her. My objective was to help her depend on Him, regardless of what her husband chose to do.

I'm always careful not to be strong about what I think a counselee should do unless the Bible takes a stand on it, so I made sure that Mary knew when I was giving my opinion and when what I said was out of God's Word. I made it clear that whatever she decided, she was responsible for the results and would have to live with her decision.

One day she asked me if I thought God could change her husband's heart and bring him back to her. I said, "Yes, He is able to do that, but He is more interested that you learn to know and trust Jesus. Then, no matter what your husband does, you will always know He is with you."

As her trust in God grew, Mary became calm and poised; her panic became peace. She began looking at life through God's eyes and began to view Him as her rock, a safe haven in the storm. She learned that God could keep her from falling apart even though her husband wasn't changing his hurtful behavior. She came to a new understanding that God would be with her in her future, even if her husband was not, and that He is enough.

The KTC asks for God's guidance, attempts to meet the felt needs of hurting people, and seeks to "lance the boil" of pain. Then she takes them to Jesus and believes for them until they can believe for themselves. The healing and restoration come from Him.

THINGS TO DO IN YOUR FIRST COUNSELING SESSION

Always meet a counselee face to-face for your first session. Many counselees are aware only of their felt need and cannot articulate the real problem they are facing. However, their body language, facial expressions, and tone of voice can reveal that they may be hiding something or that they are unaware of something. This happens because they may be unsure of whether they can trust you or feel safe with you. Watch their eyes and other unspoken responses, such as wringing hands, clenched teeth, tears, hands balled into fists, tightly crossed arms and legs, and so on.

Ask her when she invited Jesus into her heart. Her answer can help you determine your starting point and how you will approach her.

Ask her what her expectations are for the time with you. When you know what she expects, you can ascertain whether or not you can help her.

Seek to determine her level of desire to grow and change. If you discern that she is not willing to put energy into growing and making changes in her life, you can prevent a fruitless, potentially long-term commitment before it starts.

Listen carefully; do not jump to conclusions. It is important that a person feels that her problems have been heard.

When she has told you what she needs to say, pray with her. As you talk to God about her, use her name and those of the others involved in the problem. (If you have trouble remembering details, take notes during the session so that you can cover her concerns thoroughly.) When she hears her name and personal burdens being lifted to the Father, she will feel encouraged.

When people have problems, praying is often the last thing they feel like doing. They come for counseling wanting to know what to do. But at times the *only* solution to their dilemma *is* prayer; nothing can be done apart from a miracle. Prayer doesn't always provide tangible comfort because it can seem like a passive, simplistic answer, but you can encourage your counselees to stand on the truth of the Scripture.

Acts 10:1-4 tells about Cornelius, a Gentile who was hungry for God and who prayed to Him continually. As far as we know, he had never really heard the gospel, but he knew that there was a true and living God and followed everything he knew to do to please Him. The Bible says that the Lord appeared to him and told him that his prayers had "ascended as a memorial before God" (verse 4). God was saying, "You are building a monument of prayer, a work of enduring significance." When you pray for a counselee, you are constructing a prayer memorial, prayer upon prayer, brick upon brick.

Assure your counselee that every prayer that has *ever* been prayed for her or her loved ones is before God. Each prayer is part of a memorial that will never be lost, whether or not she sees the answer in her lifetime. God's Word tells us that He keeps all of our prayers: "Another angel came and stood at the altar, holding a golden censer; and much incense was given to him, so that he might add it to *the prayers of all the saints* on the golden altar which was before the throne. And the smoke of the incense, with the prayers of the saints, went up before God out of the angel's hand" (Revelation 8:3-4, emphasis mine). Our prayers go up like incense before God.

Clarify your boundaries. Let her know if and when she can call you at home. For example, I tell counselees that my evenings are reserved for my husband and that I take emergency phone calls only during that time. I tell them when they can call me during the day and that I welcome their calls. (For help on how to respond when someone calls you on the phone, see pages 71–72.)

Decide by the end of the session if you will give a counselee another appointment. It may be that you do not need to meet again because her problem will not require more sessions, or you may sense that you cannot help her or that she is unwilling to change.

If you need to meet with someone more than once, *clarify the frequency, time, and place that you will meet for a counseling session.* I always prefer a face-to-face encounter, but if after the first time it's difficult for her to meet with you, set up a regular time for counseling with her over the phone.

the bottom line of most problems

When Carolyn came to see me, her marriage was in trouble. Her struggles with her husband were seemingly insurmountable. I had difficulty pinpointing the root of the problem until we began to talk about the other men in her life (her father, brother, uncle, pastor, former boyfriends, and so on). Carolyn told me about a painful experience she'd had with an uncle. She had carried the pain and hurt for many years, and those emotional wounds had festered. Her unhappiness from the past was affecting her relationship with her husband. Because Carolyn had not forgiven her uncle, she had unconsciously projected her pain on the most important person in her life. But the cause of her marital struggles was so subtle that she did not recognize it.

Carolyn wasn't aware of what was going on inside her, because she had stuffed her pain down deep into her subconscious. She was like the person who once said to me, "I didn't know what to do with my emotional garbage, so I found a place down in my spirit and put it there." Why do we push things down into our subconscious? Because we think that is the only way we can survive and get on with our lives. An attitude like this might work for a while—until we have more garbage to stuff down. It's not very pleasant and slowly it begins to mount up and become ugly.

After many years of being a KTC, I've learned that a lack of forgiveness is the root of most problems. In almost every problem situation, after peeling off the layers of grief and distress, I find a wounded spirit or an unresolved resentment. Usually, it is the result of a hurt that hasn't been dealt with or a pain that hasn't been relinquished to God.

If we don't take care of our hurts right away and forgive those who hurt us, resentment will build. In time it may manifest itself as some other problem, as it did with Carolyn. This is true for us as KTCs as well as for the women we counsel.

MY OWN NEED TO FORGIVE

I'll never forget the experience that taught me how easy it is for all of us to be blind in this area. At the time, if you had asked me if everything was right regarding my relationships with others, I would have answered yes with a clear conscience. But God began to point out a hidden area in my life when I received a postcard from some friends who live on the East Coast. It said, "We're coming to Oregon, and we want to see you." As I read the words, my heart dropped to my shoes. I did *not* want these people to come to our home.

Many years before, our family had stayed in the home of these friends. I went down to the basement to do laundry, and when I returned upstairs, I discovered that everyone had gone for a walk except the host. He made a pass at me. He didn't hurt me, but I thought, *What a jerk! I'm not only married, but a Christian, and a missionary too!* I decided I would have nothing more to do with him. For twenty years, I had been able to steer clear of him, but now he and his wife were coming to stay in our home.

Hospitality is sacred to me, and retracting our long-standing invitation to this couple was not an option. But because their arrival was a long way off, I put the postcard aside and forgot about it. Then one night some dear friends from California, Brenda and Marty, were visiting us when the phone rang. It was the couple from the East Coast, calling to say that they were arriving the next day. I said, "We'll see you tomorrow," and hung up the phone.

Brenda, who knows me very well, said, "What's wrong, Muriel?"

"Oh, there's nothing wrong," I answered flippantly.

As we washed the dishes, I was unusually quiet, and Brenda said, "I think you'd better tell me what's going on."

"Oh, it's just a stupid incident that happened twenty years ago, and I've forgiven him."

That night, as I was trying to sleep, I kept thinking about what I'd told Brenda. *I've forgiven him. I've forgiven him!* My words seemed to be mocking me. *What's wrong, Lord?* I prayed.

His still, small voice spoke to my heart, "Muriel, you haven't forgiven him or you wouldn't dislike him so much."

Lord, please forgive me. I have held this in my heart for a long time without realizing it. I lay in the quietness, savoring the sweet healing of God's forgiveness. Then I prayed, *God, I forgive him.* I needed to be forgiven first, before I could extend it to him.

As KTCs we must have our hearts clean; we need to be up-to-date on our own forgiveness issues. As you read this chapter, ask the Holy Spirit to make you aware if there is anyone you need to forgive. In His time He will focus on any hidden areas you may need to work on. Do not worry; God is faithful.

SIGNS OF UNFORGIVENESS

To detect the problem of unforgiveness in a counselee (or yourself), ask the following questions:

- Is there someone whom you feel a dislike or hatred for? A strong negative feeling toward a person is a clue that there is something going on deep in your heart.
- Are you experiencing any uncommon anger?
- Are you feeling overwhelming fear?
- Have you had any unusual emotional outbursts such as ugly comments, unexplained tears, or yelling?
- Do you feel bitterness or resentment toward someone?
- Do you have constant turmoil in your heart?
- Are you resisting something or someone?

If she answers yes to any of the above, she probably has some forgiveness work to do.

When we are hurt, the last thing we want to do is to forgive those who have wounded us — we may even want to hurt them! But Jesus had some strong words to say about the importance of forgiveness. As KTCs we need to understand what the Bible says about forgiveness so that we can teach it to others.

WHAT DOES GOD'S WORD SAY ABOUT FORGIVENESS?

When Peter asked Jesus how many times he should forgive, the Lord told him seventy times seven. By His answer, Jesus was saying, "You *always* forgive, no matter how many times you've been wronged, so don't keep track."

Then He went on to tell a parable about a king and two of his servants (see Matthew 18:21-35). One of the slaves owed the king ten thousand talents. In Jesus' story, the king represents God and the slave that owed the talents represents us. Why did Jesus choose the amount of ten thousand? Because during biblical times this amount was "big bucks." A talent was what one man could earn in a year's time. The slave could not have paid off his debt in a lifetime; it would have taken him ten thousand years. Jesus' point is that when we sin, we owe God a huge debt—one we can't pay back, no matter how pale or insignificant our sin seems to us. We may be astounded by that thought if we feel we have never done anything really bad. However, remember that the greatest sin is independence from God. Proverbs 3:6 calls us to dependence: "In all your ways acknowledge Him." Can any of us ever say that we have *never* operated independently from God? No. This makes us debtors to Him.

When the slave was confronted about his debt, he said to the king, "Have patience with me and I will repay you everything"(Matthew 18:26). He knew, on some level, that he could never repay the money, but his response was very human. Most of us do something similar: We unconsciously try to pay for our sin, despite God's forgiveness. It is as if we say, "What Jesus did is not enough, so I have to add to it." We want to pay own our way. Such an attitude insults God and mocks the sacrifice His Son made.

If we *could* have paid for our sins, God would have let us. But because we can't, He sent His Son to pay the ultimate sacrifice for our sins—something we could not do for ourselves.

When God forgives us, that's it. We are forgiven, set free. The king excused the slave's debt; it was forgiven, wiped out. The burden of a lifetime had been lifted. I can hardly imagine how this man felt when he walked out of the presence of the king. Whew! A huge weight rolled off his shoulders; the sky must have seemed bluer and the grass greener.

Then he saw a man who owed him a hundred denarii. One denarius was the equivalent of one day's wage, so this was a sizable debt, but repayable with three or four months of steady labor. The forgiven slave probably thought, *I could use that money,* so he went up to the guy and demanded what was due him. He had already forgotten what it felt like to be forgiven. When we refuse to forgive those who have hurt us, we too show that we have forgotten that we have been forgiven. Like the slave, we can even become self-righteous toward others.

The debtor sang the very song that the forgiven slave had sung to the king: "Have patience with me and I will repay you" (verse 29). The forgiven one grabbed the other around the throat and threw him in prison. Other servants, who knew of the king's great mercy, saw the injustice and reported it to the king.

The king summoned the first slave, who had been forgiven so much, and said, "You wicked slave, I forgave you all that debt because you pleaded with me. Should you not also have had mercy on your fellow slave, in the same way that I had mercy on you?" (verses 32-33). And in anger the king had him tortured until he paid back everything he owed. When Jesus finished the parable, He made the application to Peter as well as to us, "My heavenly Father will also do the same to you, if each of you does not forgive his brother from your heart" (verse 35).

Is He really talking about us, His forgiven children? Yes. When we are unwilling to forgive and obey God's command, we put ourselves in prison. I believe some of the torturers referred to in verse 34 are anger, bitterness, guilt, hate, fear, and the inability to forgive ourselves. Forgiveness is the way we escape these tormentors.

Jesus' stand on forgiveness is an uncompromising one: "But if you do not forgive men their sins, your Father will not forgive your sins" (Matthew 6:15, NIV). That doesn't seem fair, does it? Why does God seem to make His forgiveness conditional? I believe it's because He knows how terribly destructive unforgiveness is. What appears to be a condition on His forgiveness is actually a demonstration of His love. Bitterness and resentment are like a red-hot coal in a person's heart. They burn irreparable holes. Scripture says that bitterness defiles many (see Hebrews 12:15). The destruction unforgiveness unleashes in a person's heart and life is deadly and spills over onto others. God's commandment to us to forgive was *not* given out of the meanness of His heart, nor was it meant to make life hard for us. Its purpose is *to set us free.*

In the past several years I have seen many books and magazine articles written by secular counselors, touting the value of forgiveness. Their premise is that bitterness is not good for us. They are right. Unforgiveness is not healthy for heart, soul, or body. Where these experts miss the mark is that their approach revolves around the offended person. The beautiful fact of forgiveness for the believer is that, first and foremost, we experience forgiveness from God. He then frees us to forgive others, because we can give up to Him what we feel and what we think should happen to our offender.

When we accept Christ into our hearts and He comes to live in us, we become His representatives. The Bible calls us His "ambassadors" (2 Corinthians 5:20). A friend of mine is the wife of an ambassador to a country in South America. One day she told me that once she steps foot outside her country, she "becomes" her country to everyone she encounters. This role impacts the way she dresses, talks, and relates to people. As Christ's ambassadors, we represent Him to those who don't know Him. The reason Jesus came to earth was to forgive. When we fail to reflect the heart and character of Christ before others, we misrepresent Him.

HELPING HER UNDERSTAND FORGIVENESS

When you discern that the woman you're counseling has a forgiveness problem, ask her, "Do you really want healing from your problem? Do you want to be free? I'm hearing something that makes me think you may need to forgive. Are you willing to work at that?" If she says yes, you can walk her through the steps to forgiveness.

If she holds out and says she's not sure, it may be that she misunderstands what forgiveness is.

Forgiveness Is Not Reconciliation

Some synonyms for the word *forgive* are "pardon," "excuse," "absolve."[1] Forgiveness is the act of one that has been offended or wronged. It lifts punishment and consequences from the offender. There are many people who think that forgiveness means to reestablish the broken relationship. I believe they have combined forgiveness with reconciliation, but these are two different things. We can always choose to forgive, because we are in control of our own will. However, we may not be able to choose reconciliation because the other person may not be open to it. In addition, reconciliation can be dangerous and inappropriate if the offenders continue in their ungodly, destructive ways, causing more injury and damage.

Forgiveness Is Not Condoning

Many people think that forgiving means condoning what has been done—by forgiving they absolve the offender of all responsibility for the hurt that has been inflicted on them. When Jesus forgives us our sins, He is not saying that our sins are okay. Our sin is definitely unacceptable—that is why He had to die—yet He still forgives us. Forgiveness is saying, "I take you to the foot of the cross, I lay you down, and I release you to the Lord Jesus."

For Jesus' sake we forgive the one who has hurt us; it's an issue of *obedience.* Instead of absolving the offender, we give over to God the responsibility to judge that person (see Romans 12:19). Forgiving for Jesus' sake wraps us in the joy and love of restored relationship with Him, making it no longer difficult.

Forgiveness Is Not Forgetting

Humanly, we cannot forget. In their book *Bold Love,* Drs. Dan Allender and Tremper Longman III state, "The only way for the 'forgive-and-forget mentality' to be practiced is through radical denial, deception, or pretense."[2] What we read, see, and hear goes down on record in our minds. Our mind has no delete key. That's why it is so important to guard ourselves from the input we receive. It all goes into our subconscious and stays there forever.

But if we can't forget, how do we know when we are healed? We are healed from the offense when we can think about that person or situation and it has no more power to make us angry or hurt.

However . . .

Forgiveness Is Not Instant Healing

Often when we forgive, we expect the pain to go away *now*. But that rarely happens. Even though we have removed the source of our pain through forgiveness, the actual healing can take time. Keep in mind that our emotional wounds don't necessarily heal any more quickly than our physical ones.

When my husband had his gall bladder removed, the doctor told him that he might have the same pain after the surgery for a period of months, maybe up to a year. He warned Norm about getting discouraged. Not long after his surgery, Norm came to me and said, "The doctor made a terrible mistake. He took out the wrong thing! I am still hurting. He didn't get to the bottom of the problem." I reminded him of what the doctor had told him, and we decided not to worry. One morning he woke up and said, "You know, that awful pain is gone." Just as Norm needed to be patient with his pain after his surgery, we need to be patient with the pain after we have forgiven someone. The offense may still have power over us for some time, but that power will go away if we leave the offense in Jesus' hands.

Forgiveness Is Not a Process; It's a Decision

Forgiveness is an act of the will; healing is the process. God's Word tells us to love our enemies and pray for our persecutors (see Matthew 5:44). We're told to feed them (see Romans 12:20) and to love one another (see

1 John 4:7). But nowhere in the Bible does it say to do these things if we *feel* like it. It simply tells us to do them. Why? Because if we wait until we feel like it, we'll never do them. We don't always want to forgive, *but Christ in us always does.* We have to choose to forgive with our will.

If your counselee is still unsure about forgiving someone who has wounded her, ask her what benefit she is receiving from not forgiving that person. What is she gaining by not letting go of the offense? Your counselee may surprise herself when she articulates the reasons she doesn't want to release the offenses into God's hands. One woman told me, "If I don't forgive my husband, I don't have to be nice to him. And I don't have to sleep with him. My mother and my friends sympathize with me when I talk about how awful he's been, and I won't be able to do that if I forgive him." You can gently point out that unwillingness to forgive is self-serving and self-pleasing, rather than God-honoring.

When a counselee says she wants to forgive, *you* can walk her through the steps of forgiveness.

Forgiveness Involves Four Steps

1. *Agree* with God that we need to forgive.

2. *Decide* to do it. We may agree that we *should* forgive, but if we stop there we will get stuck in step 1. We make this decision with our will; we may never feel like it.

3. *Acknowledge* who we have to forgive and *state how we feel* about it. It is helpful to write down the incidents and our feelings, and then, in prayer, turn them over to God. For example: "Dear Lord, You know how my father hurt me and made me feel that I was not important and that I was a disappointment to him. I feel so hurt by his treatment of me and I feel helpless to change it. Lord, I want to forgive my father and I choose to do that. I ask You to heal my wounded heart." Recognizing and giving up our hurt over a situation is just as important as releasing the person through forgiveness.

4. *Act out* forgiveness with our behavior, and our emotions (feelings) will follow. The world says, "If you don't feel like doing something, don't do it, because it's not honest." If I operated like that I wouldn't get much done! I never feel like cleaning my house, but I do it because it gets dirty. I choose to do it, and after I've cleaned it, I'm glad I did. I've learned a secret: If I operate with my will, my emotions will eventually follow. But if I follow my feelings, my will goes along.

Let me show you what I mean. Every morning when the alarm goes off, my will and my emotions have an argument.[3] My will says, "You've got to get up. You have to go to work today." My emotions respond, "Oh, no, I can't. I don't feel good." I never feel well in the morning. Now I have a decision to make. Am I going to stay in bed or get up? If I stay in bed, my will stays in bed too. So I get up with my will, go to the bathroom, and brush my teeth. My emotions still protest. It is only after I take a shower, drink a cup of tea, and start moving around that my emotions catch up with my will and I'm a whole person. We do something similar when we choose to forgive. We use our will, for Jesus' sake, because He asks us to, and sooner or later our emotions follow.

After going through the steps to forgiveness, one woman told me, "I have been in such an ugly place because of guilt, shame, and anger that I was getting desperate. Now that I have dealt with all that junk, I feel like I've emerged from a long dark tunnel and I'm finally hopeful!"

After a counselee has forgiven the person who hurt her, she may need to consider other issues, such as, do I confront the person who offended me? When do I do it? What do I do about the person I live with who hurts me all the time? You will find ways to deal with those issues in part 2.

FREEDOM AT LAST

I met Judy Wortley at a mother-daughter conference. She told me the incredibly sad story of how her son, Mike, was murdered—stabbed fifty times by drug dealers. Then, in the following months, her husband, Jon, abandoned her and their children. The following, in Judy's own words, is her story of healing.

Forgiveness? How many times do I have to forgive, and how many people? Yes, I made a decision to forgive the boys that killed Mike, but Jon?

Jon had pierced me through with the poison of his bitterness a million times in the last three years. He had violated me, stomped on me, called me every name in the world, been with multiple women, divorced me, left me financially uncared for. How could I forgive?

When I came to Muriel for help, she listened intently as I relayed the traumas of my life: my mother's suicide, Mike's murder, and Jon's exit from the family. Then she wisely asked if she could take me through an exercise in forgiveness. I agreed.

She began by saying, "Let's imagine on the floor between us is a big wooden crate. I want you to think about your relationship with Jon. Start from the beginning. Start with the first time you met in junior high school, and then your dating during those high school years. Think deeply about any way in which he hurt you during that time."

There were many hurts that came to mind, even in the beginning of our relationship. "Can you list them out in your mind?" she asked. I could think of many times he hurt me or treated me with disrespect. "Put them all in the crate," she said. Muriel marched me up and down the memories of my life with Jon. She said, "This is not an easy exercise, but it is crucial in your ability to go on with your life. You must forgive completely, in order for your emotions to be healed. Have you got them all put in the box?"

"Now, pretend you have a hammer and very large nails. Nail the lid on the box," she said. In my mind's eye, I could imagine the nails and my pounding each one into the lid so it could never be opened again.

"Drag, pull, push, or shove this crate up the hill to the Cross of Calvary. Put a rope around it if you need to. Place it at the foot of the cross," Muriel instructed.

I thought this would be an easy task, but hypothetically speaking, the box was heavy. Finally, I felt like I had laid it at the foot of the Cross.

"Okay, I want you to pray now and tell Jesus you give Him all these hurts as a gift—a lifetime of hurts. Tell Him you forgive Jon and any others involved. Ask the Lord to give you freedom."

So I audibly prayed, "Dear Lord, I thought I understood forgiveness. I thought I understood being devastated by pain with Mike's death. I realize this is even harder for me. I do forgive Jon, because you ask me to, not because I feel like it or because he deserves it. Lord, help me. Give my emotions back to me. Teach me to live a lifestyle of forgiveness. Father, I give these hurts to you. Help me to never take them back."

We embraced in tears. "Every time Satan tempts you to take the lid off and begin reliving the hurts, remind him it is in the box and you gave it all to Jesus," were her parting words.

An enormous burden was lifted from my shoulders. I didn't need to carry Jon's bitterness with me.

Forgiveness brings freedom. Bitterness brings bondage. Making a choice to forgive is like opening a door. Freedom hinges on our choice to forgive. Jon was in bondage, a self-made prison. His inability to forgive our son's assailants, his unwillingness to forgive God and his unwillingness to ask forgiveness for himself combined with the guilt he was bearing placed him in unbearable bondage.

Giving all my hurts to Jesus was, perhaps, the most significant thing that had happened on my road to a life of freedom.

I was learning to live one minute at a time.

I had to constantly say, "Lord, I give you this minute; free my mind for the next five minutes. Let me concentrate only on you and your strength. Don't let me think about Jon or my circumstances, but only you. I give all my hurt to you. Free me from my own thought process."

My best friend became the Word of God. Memorizing Scripture soothed the aching loneliness. Memorization gave control of my mind to the Holy Spirit allowing it to rest from turmoil. The Lord was my partner.[4]

God helped Judy make the difficult decision to forgive, and He helped her through the process of healing. Today she is a radiant, beautiful person. He can help you guide others to forgiveness, and you will find Him faithful to work in your heart as well.

The following chapter shows what God wants to do in the life of a believer, even through the most painful situation. When we understand why God permits heartaches to touch our lives, it makes it easier to release those who have hurt us into God's hand.

when the heartache seems unexplainable

Life is full of tragedy. Christians sometimes lose their jobs, get cancer, and suffer horrible accidents. Men and women who walk with God sometimes become casualties of war, leaving behind families without spouses, mothers, fathers. Why?

The Bible raises a lot of "why" questions. Why did God allow Cain to murder Abel? Cain was the wicked one; Abel was righteous. Stephen was a lovely Christian (with a face like an angel, according to Acts 6:15), yet God permitted evil men to smash his face and body with stones. Why did He let that happen? Hebrews 11, known to most of us as the "faith chapter," lists many feats of faith accomplished by God's servants. But the last part of the chapter tells us of many terrible tragedies that befell His people. Some were cut in half, others burned, and others stoned. Many of them were not delivered!

I repressed these questions for years because I couldn't reconcile them with what I knew about God's love. I was afraid that if I examined my questions too closely, I would be disappointed in God. I did not want to find that He could not measure up to my expectations.

But in order to trust God and look to Him for the future, we must release the why of tragedy. I believe we have reached the deepest level of spiritual maturity when we can trust God and His sovereign purpose in tragedy (see levels of spiritual maturity on pages 83–85). If you can do this for your own life, you will know how to help when your counselee asks you "why" questions like these.

MY JOURNEY TO TRUST

I was catapulted into seeking to understand God's sovereignty and His purposes in tragedy when I was a young wife and mother. Norm and I were thirty-five, with two beautiful children. All was well and we were energetic, busy, and happy in our work as missionaries.

But something happened that shook my world while we were attending a conference several hours away from our home, high in the mountains of Taiwan. Before the evening meeting Norm decided to swim in a nearby lake. A twelve-year-old boy from another family swam with him. Unknown to them, both were bitten by a mosquito carrying deadly Japanese encephalitis B. Three days after the conference, much to the shock and sorrow of the missionary community, the boy died.

Two weeks later, Norm lay in the hospital, close to death. I was terrified. The doctor told me the first day that he had only a 30 percent chance to live. The next day, the prognosis was death. Norm was unconscious, and although they were doing all they could, the doctors gave us no hope. Dr. Dick Hillis, the director of our mission organization, flew in from the United States to conduct my husband's funeral.

The night the doctor told me that Norm was dying, I felt stunned and sickened. I returned to our home, shut myself in our room, and lay on the floor for a long time. I knew I had to trust God and keep my faith in Jesus, whether Norm lived or died. But how could I do that? We were childhood sweethearts and I loved him more than my own life.

Somewhere in the back of my mind came the word *relinquishment,* "Give him up to Jesus." I thought, *I could* never *give him up!* Then, I believe, the Holy Spirit gently led me to see that I *could* give my husband over to Him because He always does what is right. I wanted my way, but I don't always know what is best. With my will I began to give each part of our life together over to God. Norm was my friend and lover, the father of my children, and my future. As I let go of each part, God brought peace to my heart.

I felt very weak, but the Lord gave strength and courage for each step I had to take. Even though Norm had been unconscious for a week, he thrashed about so strongly that they had to tie him down. Then, for three days he lay dead-still. The doctor came to me with a very sad face and told me that he believed that my husband would live, but that he had extensive brain damage and would never recognize our children or me. Norm would not be able to work or even feed himself.

This news was even worse than the prospect of death, but 2 Samuel 22:29-33 sustained me: "As for God, His way is perfect. He is my shield and my strong fortress. Who else is a rock besides our God? And He makes my way perfect" (my paraphrase). The Word of God gave me comfort. I became convinced that no matter what the outcome, God *said* that His way was perfect and that He would make my way perfect. The only peace I got was when I believed that.

When Norm suddenly awakened, the doctors were shocked that he had no brain damage. However, it took him a year to recover his strength. Through the unexplainable heartache of Norm's illness and long recovery, God taught me that when I was cut off from any other hope except Him, He was trustworthy.

For that reason, I want to show you what I learned from God's Word, particularly the book of Job, about how God works through unexplainable heartaches and how we should respond.

HOW DOES GOD WORK
THROUGH HEARTACHE?

Job was a very wealthy Middle Eastern landowner with large numbers of donkeys, sheep, camels, and cattle. He also had many servants, who no doubt lived with him and his family. Life was good—and then one day Job received a tremendous blow. One-third of his servants, whom he knew and loved, had been slaughtered by the Sabeans, slashed to death with swords (see Job 1:13-15). On top of this devastating news, Job learned that he had taken an enormous economic hit with the slaughter of his cattle and donkeys. The messenger was still delivering this message when more bad news arrived. A second messenger told Job, "The fire of God fell from heaven and burned up the sheep and the servants and consumed them, and I alone have escaped to tell you" (verse 16).

I believe the fire that fell from heaven was lightning. Who controls the elements? God does; they are a gift from Him. Would God allow Satan to take something that is His and use it against His child? Jesus said that God "sends rain on the righteous and the unrighteous" (Matthew 5:45). He allows nature, His gift, to impact everyone. The confidence that we can have when natural disasters touch us is that God has an overarching purpose for good in our lives.

While the second man was still delivering his message, a third one came and announced that the Chaldeans had raided all Job's camels and killed the servants attending them (see Job 1:17). No doubt, Job had to break the news to their wives, children, and parents that they were dead. The loss was very personal because Job had probably gone to their weddings, celebrated the births of their children, and attended their funerals. What an enormous tragedy! On top of the human loss, Job's camels had been stolen. The fact that he owned camels meant that he was probably a merchant. With that third blow, he lost all his sources of income.

When I think about the next part of Job's story, I feel sick. God didn't even spare Job's family. And it wasn't just one child, but all of them in one sweep. A great wind, like a tornado, struck the house, lifted it off the foundation, and all of them lost their lives (see verses 18-19). It's beyond belief what God permitted Satan to do.

Yet Job's story helps us lift our eyes off our circumstances and onto God and His mysterious purposes. I believe that Scripture teaches the following truths that help us find meaning in the face of unexplainable heartache.

God Allows Those He Loves to Suffer

The scene in heaven in the first chapter of Job has always interested me. The sons of God came to report to Him and Satan tagged along. I think he had a lot of gall to show up in heaven after his attempted coup. Or maybe God summoned him; we don't know. Anyway, there he was. When the Lord asked Satan what he was doing, he said he had come from walking around on the earth. As Peter wrote, "Your adversary, the devil, prowls around like a roaring lion, seeking someone to devour" (1 Peter 5:8). Satan couldn't lie to God. He *had* been walking around, but he only told God half the story. God cut right to the heart of the issue because He knew that the Enemy was looking for someone to eat up. He asked, "Have you seen my man Job?" (Job 1:8, my paraphrase).

I think God pointed Job out because He is full of love for His children and loves to talk about them. Although God knew there was work to be done in Job's life, He was bragging on His child. My daughters are grown women, yet I still love to watch and talk about them. God is no different. His love for Job was strong.

God said that Job was blameless. I believe He meant that He saw Job as pure. It is obvious from the rest of the book that Job was far from perfect and that he had a lot to learn. But God saw Job through the eyes of love as blameless and upright. He views us the same way.

God Limits Our Suffering

Satan is known as "the father of lies" (John 8:44), but he could not lie to God. He said, "Yeah, Job's a good guy because you have protected him. Anybody would be good with a hedge around him!" (Job 1:9-11, my paraphrase). The truth of God's protection should thrill us as believers. The hedge was not for Job only; God has put it around all of His children — including you and me.

The New Testament backs up this hedge principle: "For you have died and your life is hidden with Christ in God" (Colossians 3:3). *Christ* is our hedge. We are covered with Christ and wrapped in God as well. Grasping this concept was critical for me in facing life's unexplainable heartaches. Because of what the Bible says, I know that I can rest on this truth: Nothing touches me without going through God's permission first.

Satan told God, "I cannot touch Job because of the hedge" (see Job 1:10). He wanted God to let him "have a crack" at Job (see 1:11). The Enemy believed that if he could get to him, Job would curse God. But "then the Lord said to Satan, 'Behold, all that he has is in your power, only do not put forth your hand on him.' So Satan departed from the presence of the Lord" (1:12). Wow! God placed limits on Satan. He gave him permission to go only so far and no farther.

That is true for us as well. Satan cannot touch us without God's divine permission. If we think we can't bear something, and we are facing it anyway, it is because God knows us better than we know ourselves. He *will not* give us more than we can stand (see 1 Corinthians 10:13). He places boundaries on the suffering He allows in the lives of His children.

Luke gives the New Testament counterpart to Job 1. Jesus said to Simon Peter, "Simon, Simon, behold, Satan has demanded permission to sift you like wheat; but I have prayed for you, that your faith may not fail; and you, when once you have turned again, strengthen your brothers" (22:31-32). Once again, note that Satan had to ask God's permission to touch Peter. In the same way, when you walk with God, no evil person, no illness, no car accident, no ugly or evil thing that has to do with death, pain, and suffering can touch your life, except by God's divine permission. Christ Jesus, the Hedge, protects you.

Everything that Satan does is with the purpose to destroy. His goal in sifting (testing) Peter was to annihilate his faith. In Peter's day, farmers would take big baskets of wheat outside for sifting. They would shake the hulls off the grain, and the wind would blow away the chaff and leave the inside kernel. If the grain was sifted without care, the wind came and blew everything away—both the good and bad—and ruined the harvest. Satan wanted to ruin Job's and Peter's faith, and he wants to destroy yours as well. Why would God ever let Satan do that? Does He want you to be destroyed? No!

Perhaps you are wondering if we can ever get out from behind God's hedge. Yes, we can. We don't lose Jesus, but we can step out of His light or out from under the umbrella of His blessing. That's what David did: "But the thing David had done displeased the LORD" (2 Samuel 11:27, NIV). When he went out on his porch and looked over to the place next door, he saw Bathsheba taking a bath. I do not believe that David planned that. He was simply confronted with temptation. But, as soon as he saw Bathsheba, he had to make a decision. He could have chosen to turn and go back into the palace, but he chose to stay and watch her bathe. The minute he chose to stay, he stepped out of God's light and was on his own.

Everything that happened from that moment on was not of God. God never wanted David to fall into sexual sin with Bathsheba. He did not want David to scar his life forever by murdering her husband in order to cover up what he had done. The evil David did was not God's plan, and the sin that David committed deeply marked him. He confessed his sin in Psalm 51, but it still scarred him. Both he and the following generations suffered the consequences of his stepping out from under God's protection. After his sin, David's sons showed a great deal of bitterness against him and against his God. One son raped his sister; another killed his brother and turned against his father. We must remember that David's sons made choices that led to those tragedies. David's sin may have influenced their actions, but it did not excuse them. Yet his sons could have allowed their disillusionment and disappointment in their father to drive them to God instead of away from Him.

You may ask, "David knew what he was doing, but what if I sin and don't know it?" Paul wrote in Philippians, "I press on toward the goal to win the [supreme and heavenly] prize to which God in Christ Jesus is calling us upward. So let those [of us] who are spiritually mature and full-grown have this mind *and* hold these convictions; and if in any respect you have a different attitude of mind, God will make that clear to you also" (3:14-15, AMP, emphasis mine). When we have done something wrong and do not know it, God will reveal it to us in His time. When we know to do right and do not do it, that is sin (see James 4:17). When God shows us that we have done wrong, if we refuse to deal with it, then we are out of His light because of our stubbornness, disobedience, or inability or unwillingness to step back under His protection by confessing our sin. We do not lose our salvation, but we have pulled our life out of God's hands and taken back the responsibility for it.

Suffering Makes Us More Like Christ

When we were living in Asia and I wanted to bake a cake, I had to sift the flour two or three times. The first time I'd find hair, dirt, or even stones. The second time I often got rid of lumps that were left. With each sifting the flour became finer still. I believe that the Lord allowed Satan to sift Peter in order to bring up all the "dirt and stones" in his life. Testing (sifting) shows us what is really in our hearts and how strong our faith is. My husband often says that you don't know how strong a tea bag is until you put it in hot water. Trials are meant to refine us and to show us how truly dependent and weak we are without

Him; He wants us to see that we cannot make it on our own.

The Bible tells us that "all things . . . work together for good" (Romans 8:28). Everything? If someone quotes that Scripture to you when you are in a crisis, you probably feel like punching that person in the nose. Romans 8:29 shows what God means by "good": "For those whom He foreknew, He also predestined to become conformed to the image of His Son." The good that comes from tragedy is that God is making you like Jesus. From a human perspective, good is when we feel everything is fine and we are happy. However, our happiness is not God's goal. When we know and are like Him, we experience joy in spite of what happens to us.

Job's story not only helps us understand God's purposes in life's heartaches, it also shows us how we should respond to suffering.

HOW SHOULD WE RESPOND TO HEARTACHE?

After Job received the news about the death of all of his children, he

> arose and tore his robe and shaved his head, and he fell to the
> ground and worshiped. He said,
>
>> "Naked I came from my mother's womb,
>> And naked I shall return there.
>> The LORD gave and the LORD has taken away.
>> Blessed be the name of the LORD."
>
> Through all this Job did not sin nor did he blame God.
> (Job 1:20-22)

Note *who* did all that. Job knew that all destruction originated with Satan, but he also knew that God had to give His permission. Everything that touched him had to come through God's hedge. Job knew he was not a toy of Satan; that's why he could say that God had taken all that he treasured, yet still worship.

We Need to Express Our Anguish

In Job's grief, he tore his hair, ripped his robe, and fell to the ground. His expression of agony was not a sin, nor was it blaming God. It was normal and healthy. People need to grieve their losses. It is good to cry and express anguish of heart. A woman whose husband committed suicide told me that when she learned of his death, she fainted. That is a form of grief.

Thank God for the Hard Things

Although he was in deep distress, the first thing Job did when he got himself together was worship. Worship is an attitude of total trust that is expressed in the sacrifice of thanksgiving (see Psalm 50:9-15). A sacrifice of thanksgiving seems to be a contradiction in terms. A sacrifice means suffering or a painful, costly gift. Thanksgiving is equated with gratitude. For the believer, thanksgiving goes beyond expressing appreciation. True worship—trust—is saying thank you to God for the hard things, even when we are not grateful and our heart is broken. As Paul wrote, "Always giving thanks for all things in the name of our Lord Jesus Christ to God, even the Father" (Ephesians 5:20, emphasis mine). This verse can cause us to stumble and feel angry or bewildered when we don't understand that thanksgiving, for the believer, is a *statement of trust*.

Job said, "The LORD gave and the LORD has taken away" (1:21). Why did he say that? Wasn't Satan the one who had caused Job's losses? Why would Job say that God was responsible? Because Job knew that he was in God's hedge, so he did not accept the blows as from Satan. Job's losses *did* originate with the Enemy, but by the time they touched his life, they were a part of God's purpose for him. His tragedy had to come through God's divine permission before it could touch his life.

Job's approach to his heartaches is a difficult concept to accept because it is in stark contrast to the victim mentality that permeates our society. Most of us see ourselves as victims: "My brother did this to me" or "The drunk driver was the reason" or "My pastor failed me" or "My childhood was unhappy." Satan wants us to blame and censure others in order to make us believe that evil has power over us. When we recognize that God is in control of all things concerning us (see Roman 8:28), wonderful peace can be ours *because* of the circumstances in our lives. We know that God wants to bring good out of them. He does not want us to suffer without reason. He has a plan to bring beauty from the pain in our lives. No suffering is purposeless and nothing catches Him by surprise.

Being a believer does not mean that we will experience more—or less—pain than other people. Everyone suffers. But we have a loving Father who says to us, "You are not exempt from pain, but I'll be with you, and I have a purpose in those things that I allow to touch you" (see Isaiah 43:1-7).

Sadly, I've known many Christians who turned away from God when they experienced tragedy. They stopped praying, reading the Bible, and going to church. They hold what has happened to them against God. By doing that, they allow their suffering to be used for evil. They lose their ability to trust God and others. Their joy is gone. I hear women say with bitterness, "He/she/they let me down!" Their words show that they have allowed Satan to use suffering for evil in their life, when God's plan was to bring about good.

Jesus said to Peter, "When once you have turned again . . ." (Luke 22:32). What did Jesus mean? I believe he was saying, "You have no choice over the sifting that is going on in your life, but you can let Satan turn it for evil by making you bitter or you can choose to let God turn it for good and make you like Jesus. You can pray, 'Lord, I choose to let You turn this into good in my life. I bow my knee. I give up my rights; I thank You for this. I do not appreciate it. I don't like it, but I trust You.'" This is what Hilda did.

I met Hilda after a woman called me, saying, "We have a serious situation in our church with a woman, and we can't seem to help her. Our pastor has not been able to get through to her either, and she is very despondent. Would you be willing to see her?"

During our first meeting, I asked Hilda to tell me her story. What she shared was heartbreaking. She and her husband, Pavel, had been born and raised in Eastern Europe, where Communism ruled everyone. They were in constant danger because of their Christian faith. In fact, Pavel was imprisoned several times. Because of the religious persecution they were experiencing, Hilda and Pavel decided to take their son and flee their country to save their lives. She shared with me the fascinating and harrowing story of how they escaped and slowly made their way to America. She and Pavel came to this country full of hope that the worst was behind them and that they could start a new life.

Pavel was very skilled in working with wood. In his home country he had owned his own shop, making beautiful, customized pieces of furniture. He was confident that he could make a living for his family in his adopted country. But that was not the case. Pavel applied for work time after time, place after place, but no one offered him a job. No one seemed to appreciate what he could do.

To make ends meet, Hilda found a job waiting tables, but her husband grew increasingly despondent. He felt disgraced that he could not provide for the family. Hilda tried to cheer him and love him, but despite her efforts, Pavel became even more depressed. One dark morning, she was afraid to leave him because his spirits were so low, but when he insisted she go to work, she did. When she left the house, she prayed for protection over Pavel as tears streamed down her cheeks. That morning he cleaned the house and did all the chores that he could find to do. Afterward he went down to the basement and took his life. When their teenaged son came home from school, he found his father hanging from a rope.

Hilda went on to tell me that their son became bitter and rebellious after Pavel's suicide and that he was on drugs. It was as if she had lost both her husband and son. She asked, "Why did Pavel leave me? Why didn't God help us? I have been so hurt and bewildered and have tried to live with this pain for two years. I think I cannot heal and the only way out for me now is to take my life."

Hilda and I talked for a long time about her relationship with God. I realized that she truly loved the Lord and had always wanted to please Him. I told her that I did not know why the circumstances of their life had turned out as they had but that God understood. We talked about God's mercy and how He, in His wisdom, understood Pavel and that because of this she could commit her husband to a loving God. God knew Pavel's heart and would take care of it all.

I told her, "Now God is asking you to accept His sovereignty in your life and release your whys." Hilda said that she wanted to trust Him, but didn't know how. I talked with her about the sacrifice of thanksgiving, explaining that saying thank you to God is a statement of relinquishment and trust. I knew that it would be a costly gift to give up her feelings of anger and betrayal, but I also knew that in choosing to place that kind of trust in God, Hilda would begin to heal. Trust would bring peace to her soul.

Her initial response was "I don't think I can thank God for this."

"Hilda, it has to be an act of the will to totally abandon yourself to God's sovereignty when you don't feel like it. Are you willing to offer this sacrifice?"

"I think that is what I must do now."

We knelt, weeping, as she haltingly told God, "Lord, here is my broken heart. I don't understand everything, but I am saying thank you, even for Pavel's death, because I trust you."

When we finished praying, I hugged Hilda tightly and asked if she would pray that prayer every day and keep in touch with me. "When I asked you to kneel, you were able to bow before God because you chose to trust Him with your will. That's the choice you will have to make every day."

Four months later Hilda called me. With a hopeful tone in her voice, she told me, "I am beginning to heal. I feel so different." Many months later, her son began to turn around after seeing the change in his mother and experiencing the peace in their home.

CAN GOD TAKE CARE OF ME?

Have you ever wondered, *Is God able to take care of me? Has life played a cruel joke? Can God be trusted?* I am sure that Shadrach, Meshach, and Abednego wondered the same thing. They had honored God by defying the king's orders, and they were going to be punished for it. But their answer to the king showed *who* they held on to when they were facing, literally, the hottest test of their lives: "Our God whom we serve is *able* to deliver us from the furnace of blazing fire; and He will deliver us out of your hand, O king. But *even if He does not,* let it be known to you, O king, that we are not going to serve your gods or worship the golden image that you have set up" (Daniel 3:17-18, emphasis mine).

When we face unexplainable heartaches, we can stand with these three men of faith, along with countless others, and say, "God is able to deliver me . . . but even if He does not, I will not bow to evil. I will trust Him and thank Him" (my paraphrase). Job revealed his response to the tragedies that had hit him:

> "As for me, I *know* that my Redeemer lives,
> And at the last He will take His stand on the earth.
> "*Even after my skin is destroyed,*
> Yet from my flesh *I shall see God*"
> (Job 19:25-26, emphasis mine).

Job had grown in his knowledge and trust of God in the midst of his pain.

That's what my friend, Carol King, did. A talented administrator and public speaker, Carol was a woman who sought after God's heart. Her zest for life and sense of humor often lifted my spirits. She had three grown daughters and several lovely grandbabies. When cancer took over her body, Carol suffered horribly for months. Near the end of her life, in one of our telephone conversations, she said to me, "Muriel, I am not ready to die."

Her remark concerned me. Was she not ready to meet her Maker? I asked her why.

She responded, "I haven't had enough time to offer to my beloved Lord the sacrifice of thanksgiving. When I get to heaven it will be easy to thank Him because everything will be wonderful. The difficulty of this illness is my only opportunity to worship Him in a way that costs me. I would not have chosen to have this cancer, but because I have learned to know God through it, I would not change it."

Carol, like Hilda, learned to trust God in tragedy. She had grown to know God more deeply and to understand His purposes for her unexplainable heartache. We can do the same — and when we do, we will be able to share our unbending trust with those who are experiencing deep heartache.

keeping your priorities straight

One day Susan came to me, very distressed. "My family is mad at me. I'm exhausted all the time, and everybody expects more from me than I can give!" As we talked, it became clear that Susan was a natural when it came to Kitchen Table Counseling. She found great joy in helping people and always made herself available whenever someone asked for help, which was often. As a result, she had become unbalanced in her ministry as a KTC. In her eagerness to help others, she had lost sight of herself, her own needs, and her priorities. She had diluted her strengths and energies to the point that she could not give her best to anyone.

Unless we keep our priorities straight, this can happen to any KTC. When I first began counseling women, I found myself so overburdened with the needs of those I counseled that I could not eat or enter into family activities with joy because I felt I should be praying for those I was meeting with. Then one day I realized that God was telling me, "When that person you are working with goes out of your sight, bring her to Me, leave her at My feet, and walk away, knowing that I have her in My hand. She is responsible to Me and not to you. I will follow her. You are simply a conduit for My truth." I've found that if God wants me to pray for someone when I am not with her, He will prompt my mind. When I am standing in the shower, on the way to the grocery store, or sitting at my desk, He will bring someone and her needs to my mind, and I will pray for her. As KTCs we need to remember that those we counsel have an Intercessor who sits at the right hand of God, ever making intercession for them (see Romans 8:34). We can trust God to include us in that intercession whenever He deems necessary.

Balance is one of the watchwords of the KTC. Some women are so focused on their family that they lose sight of the needs of the world. Others live on the other extreme and disregard their family. Jesus asked His disciples, "For what will it profit a man if he gains the whole world and forfeits his soul?" (Matthew 16:26). Your family is a part of your soul. Your husband and children need to be your priority over the women you are working with.

Here are some guidelines that have helped me balance my ministry with my commitments to my family and other responsibilities. If you follow these dos and don'ts, they can help you keep things in balance too.

GUARD YOUR HOME

Jesus said to His disciples, "But you will receive power when the Holy Spirit has come upon you; and you shall be My witnesses both in Jerusalem, and in all Judea and Samaria, and even to the remotest part of the earth" (Acts 1:8). Note that the power to be His witnesses comes from the Holy Spirit and that Jesus told His followers to minister first where they were—in Jerusalem. Our family is our "Jerusalem." The apostle Paul said something similar when he told older women to teach younger women to "love their husbands, to love their children, to be . . . keepers at home" (Titus 2:4-5, KJV).

To guard my home, I don't meet with a counselee there until I know her well and have confidence that she will honor my time. Instead I ask her to meet me at my office or a neutral but private location. I don't agree to meet in public places, such as restaurants, because being in public might inhibit her ability to cry and express what is going on in her heart. I've found that a parked car can be good for a private talk. In a car we can sit side by side rather than eyeball to eyeball, which can be intimidating until she gets to know me. I sometimes meet with counselees at a park, where we can be in pleasant surroundings and talk without being overheard. If a woman has young children, I often agree to meet with her at her home. This gives me control of the amount of time I spend with her.

If I feel comfortable inviting a counselee into my home, I make sure she understands my priorities. I let her know that she is important to me, but that when my husband is home, my time belongs to him. If he comes home while she is still there, I bring our conversation to a close with prayer and offer to meet with her another time. Then I stand so that she will also stand, and I walk her to the door. When I had children at home, I didn't schedule a counseling session during after-school hours. My goal then and now is to protect my family from the burdens of the women who come into my life.

If the phone rings and a counselee calls me with an urgent need when Norm is home, unless she is threatening to commit suicide I make an appointment to call or meet with her as soon as possible. I am always careful to communicate joy that she called, but then I say something like, "I can't talk right now, but I can meet with you tomorrow morning at ten o'clock," and then we agree on a location.

Other times I might say,

- "I just have five (or ten or fifteen) minutes. Tell me what's on your heart. I'd love to hear it."
- "I have to hang up now, but I'll call you back as soon as I can." Then I hang up the phone, say a prayer, and call her when it

is convenient. (If you say this to someone, be sure to call her back as you said: as soon as you can.)

- "I'm getting ready to run out the door, but I've got ten minutes before I have to leave. Tell me what is going on and let's pray before I have to go."
- "My husband will be home in just a few minutes. I can talk until then."
- "I'm so glad you called. I can't talk right now. I'll call you back as soon as I can, and in the meantime count on my prayers."

Sometimes guarding our home means setting aside our ministry as a KTC for a time. This was true for Amanda. Her daughter was desperately traumatized because of the time Amanda spent with others, so she dedicated herself almost exclusively to her family's needs, recognizing and trusting God that it was only for a period of time. Amanda's daughter, who is now in college, laughingly leaves voice messages like this one when her mom's not home: "You must be counseling somebody. Give me a call when you're done!" The season Amanda chose to invest in her Jerusalem paid rich dividends in her family relationships, and now she's free to exercise her KTC gifts once again.

BE SURE OF HER WILLINGNESS TO CHANGE

Remember the man at the pool of Bethesda in John 5:1-9? Before Jesus healed him, He asked the man if he wanted to be healed. I think Jesus asked him this question because of the lifestyle change that would be required of him after he was healed. For all we know, he had been lying around the pool, playing checkers for thirty-eight years. Did he really want to be healed and face the responsibilities of normal life?

When the crippled man said that he did want to be healed, Jesus addressed his physical need, saying, "Get up." Then He gave him a job:

"Pick up your pallet and walk" (verse 8). The man's new life required a lifestyle change. He had to be willing to do the work necessary, just as your counselee does. If she is not willing to put effort into doing a project that you've asked her to do, she will probably not be willing to make the changes that will be required for her emotional healing.

Peter tells us that those who have faith in Jesus Christ have been given "everything [they] need for life and godliness" (2 Peter 1:3, NIV). But the passage goes on to say that for this reason we are to apply all diligence in our faith (see verses 5-8). In other words, we must supply self-control to become godly, loving, and so on. Just as with the man at the pool, God supplies the power, but we must apply hard work. He will not heal us if we are not willing to participate.

If I am counseling a woman whom I suspect is not serious about changing, I see if she is willing to follow through on what I ask her to do. I assign her a project and don't meet with her again until she has done what I have asked of her. For example, Rose kept calling me to share the latest problem she had caused with her tongue. It seemed to me that her identity was wrapped up in how she always put her foot in her mouth. Because I wanted to make sure that Rose was willing to do the work required for her to heal emotionally, I said, "I'd like you to read the book of James. There is something about the tongue in each chapter. Note how these verses impact you and how they can address your current struggle. Then come back and we'll discuss your next step."

The next day Rose called, saying, "Guess what I've done now!" I stopped her and asked if she had begun the James study.

"I haven't had time," she replied.

"Then I can't help you with your tongue," I said, making sure my voice was firm but kind. "And there's no need to go over it again until you do the project. When you've done that, call and we can talk about it."

LIMIT COUNSELING SESSIONS TO ONE HOUR

I have found that usually a counselee doesn't need more than sixty minutes to explain her situation. Once in a while, if the problem is very complicated, extra time may be warranted, but this is rare. So when I agree to meet with someone, I always let her know that we will meet for only one hour and that we will schedule additional sessions if needed. I've found that if I don't limit our time to an hour, a counselee may absorb more time than I can give her.

Because of my job as a counselor at Multnomah Bible College, my office is the place where I most often talk with those I counsel. I have a clock behind the chair in which my guests normally sit. This allows me to check the time without being obvious about it. If a counselee isn't ready to leave when the time is up, I ask her how I can pray for her before she goes. When I finish praying, I stand and start walking toward the door.

If a woman asks to meet with me for more than an hour, I simply tell her that my schedule is full. I don't explain what fills it—other counseling sessions, housework, or other responsibilities. If she comes unannounced to my office (or home), I tell her, "Come on in! I've got twenty minutes to talk." If my husband is home when she drops by, I stand at the door and say, "I only have a few minutes; my husband is here." I may even walk her to her car. If I have pressing things to do, I may invite her to talk while I'm doing what I need to do. For example, "Come in and talk to me while I scrub the tub." Even though I set firm boundaries and limits, I always keep in mind that hurting people need to feel welcome. If I make them feel as if they are imposing on me, they will stop coming for help.

DO NOT COUNSEL THE OPPOSITE SEX

I have been accused of being old-fashioned and narrow-minded when I insist that men should not regularly counsel women and vice versa.

But we don't have to look far to see the wisdom of this boundary. For example, look at what happened when the New York Fire Department set up a support system for widows who had lost their firefighting husbands in the World Trade Center on September 11. According to national correspondent Jon Frankel, "At least eight firefighters have left their wives and children to start new lives with the widows of firefighters who died that fateful day."[1]

A bond can form between an emotionally needy person and the one who listens to him or her sympathetically and shows strength and tenderness. The listener, in turn, may receive understanding, admiration, appreciation, and respect — things he or she may not be getting at home. When a man and a woman are alone, without other people around, they enter an environment in which it is easy to step over the line into emotional or even sexual intimacy. Praying together about a common concern fosters intimacy, and it is dangerous for members of the opposite sex to enter into that kind of one-on-one communication.

I do my best never to put myself in a place of temptation or where my motives might be misunderstood. If a man asks me to meet with him for help with a problem, I find another man to counsel him.

PROTECT YOURSELF FROM THE HEAVINESS OF OTHERS' BURDENS

At the end of a day of counseling, I can be very heavy-hearted. After all, in the course of each day, I hear horrible language and life stories that are not edifying. The weight of the problems I hear will wear me down unless I keep focused on the principles of Mark 2:1-12 (see chapter 3). I often remind myself that my responsibilities as a KTC are to ask God for guidance, lance the boil of her pain, meet her felt needs, take her to Jesus, believe for her, and help her to become independently dependent on God.

As a young KTC trying to help people, I found myself carrying the anguish of others into my home life. If a woman poured out her heart about a cruel, abusive husband, it was difficult for me not to be mad at my own husband. Just listening to her story could affect me negatively.

I asked God how I could keep the filth and sin that I heard from dragging me down. He showed me through a story I heard about a man who worked with drug addicts and gang members day in and day out. This man felt poisoned by the dark problems he dealt with each day. He would return home so shell-shocked that he could not participate in family activities, something he believed God would have him do. Then God spoke to him through Mark 16:18, which says, "They will pick up serpents . . . it will not hurt them." He realized that it was as if he had been bitten by the evil that touched him everyday. He felt that God was telling him to take a few minutes every evening to pray and ask Him to clean the ugliness from his mind and spirit and fill him with peace. He started doing this and found that he was able to be the father and husband he wanted to be.

After I heard that story, I started asking God to clean out what I had heard that day and to fill me with peace. This, along with the next point, has helped to protect me from being weighed down by what I hear every day.

RESTORE YOUR SPIRIT

Even though great multitudes were gathering to hear Jesus and to be healed of their sicknesses, He would often slip away to the wilderness and pray (see, for example, Luke 5:15-16). His walk with the Father was His first priority.

We need to follow His example in this. We cannot help others unless we are walking in intimacy with Him, learning more of Him, listening to His voice, and gaining His discernment and wisdom for our life and for those we touch.

We wouldn't think of driving our car on an empty tank, but it is very easy to allow our spiritual tank to run on empty while attempting to care for the needs of others. To keep your spiritual tank full, do the following.

Spend Time with God Each Day

Just as dressing is a critical part of my preparation for each day, so is my time with God. I cannot help others if I am not "clothed" in Him. I can care much better for others and myself out of a full relationship with God.

For years I struggled with having a morning quiet time before the demands of the day crowded in. I have learned that *when* I meet with God isn't important; what's important is doing so. Before I was married, I spent time with God before going to bed each night. Now that my evenings belong to my husband, I choose to spend time in the Word at other times of the day. A friend of mine is on medication that makes her sleepy. The only time she is alert is when she is eating her lunch, so she has her devotions while she eats. Another friend uses her children's daily naptime to pray and read the Bible.

I said in chapter 3 that one of the guiding principles for a KTC is to ask God for guidance or to seek a word from Him. God often guides me through my daily Bible reading. I expect Him to speak to me there, for as Hebrews 11:6 says, "Without faith it is impossible to please Him, for he who comes to God must believe that He is and that He is a rewarder of those who seek Him."

Do Things That Help You Care for Yourself

Jesus was the most balanced person who ever lived. He took time to have lunch with friends and attend social events. He went hiking, boating, and fishing. We can follow His example and take some time for restoration.

What activities restore you? Ask yourself, What would give me a peace and confidence out of which to minister? It could be something as big as organizing your home or as simple as wiping down your refrigerator. It might be exercising regularly, reading a good book, window shopping, having lunch with a friend or a movie date with your husband, doing a craft project, painting your nails, or making your bed. Sometimes taking the time to iron a shirt, go for a walk, or scrub the bathroom can be the thing that frees us to feel better about who we are so that we can reach out to others.

I find restoration in having a change of scenery, doing something completely different from my daily life. I love to eat out and go to operas, concerts, and museums. I also enjoy entertaining guests and planning topics to talk about that give fresh mental stimulation. One time I invited a group of girlfriends to come for Japanese food. I asked each one to bring along her favorite pajamas or lounging outfit to wear at dinner while I cooked for them at the table. Sometimes my husband and I have friends over for dinner and a funny movie. We look for anything that helps us laugh. Laughter is so reviving.

One of my daughters takes mini-vacations by grabbing a diet cola and a magazine and taking a leisurely bubble bath. Another woman I know treats herself with a wander through a discount store or a couple of garage sales. (Watch out for extravagance; doing something beyond your means can deplete rather than restore.) What restores you? When you spend time replenishing yourself, you will have more energy to care for others.

USE YOUR GOD-GIVEN WISDOM

If you have been a KTC for long, you will have developed your own list of guidelines. The ones in this chapter are *not* definitive. Ask God to show you what you need to be doing. Be careful to follow what you have learned and observed from others' lives in order to be a balanced woman of God as you seek to touch others in His name.

moving on to
spiritual maturity

When a woman meets with me initially, she is usually in crisis and wants answers to a specific problem. But once she has addressed that critical need (whether in one counseling session or a series of sessions), we don't meet again unless another situation arises. However, some women, after dealing with a crisis, express a desire to continue meeting with me so that I can help them grow spiritually. This was the case for Laura.

THE CRISIS

Laura came to see me soon after Freshman Orientation. When I asked her to tell me about herself, she said, "My Sunday school teacher helped me ask Jesus into my heart when I was eight years old. I grew up going to church. I have two older brothers and everyone in my family is a Christian. My mother is involved in every women's activity the church has going, and everyone thinks she is a wonderful Christian.

"Ever since I was a little girl, Mom has taken me to beauty contests. We have traveled to all kinds of places for competitions. I have never had

79

an interest in those things and don't even enjoy them, but the only time my mom ever shows me any love is when I am successful at a pageant or doing something that she can brag about. Because of that, I feel as if I have to do things I don't want to do in order to have a relationship with her. Even though I try to make my mom happy, she is always disappointed in me. I try and try, and can never get anything right.

"Mom does all sorts of things for the church, but she has never talked to me about God. She has not shown me how to live as a Christian. The only time I feel she pays attention to me or cares what I do is when we are shopping for clothes, working on makeup, or trying to make a good impression in some social setting."

Laura shook and sobbed as she talked about her mother's disappointment in her. She continued, "Every time I go away from home and return, I think things have changed, that this time she will love me for who I am. Within a few minutes of getting in the door, I am always disappointed and hurt. I want to be able to get over this before I go home at Thanksgiving. My mother is not happy that I came to a Bible college, so I already have that strike against me."

Laura needed to be able to move beyond the disappointment and hurt she felt when she was around her mother, as well as grieve that her mother was not who she wanted her to be.

DEALING WITH THE CRITICAL ISSUE

When I was sure that Laura had finished telling me all that was on her heart, I told her, "If you keep hoping and longing for your mother to change, you will be re-wounded every time she does not treat you the way you wish she would. When you can come to terms with who your mother really is and when you recognize that she will not be the ideal mother you want her to be, then you will be free to enjoy her on the level that she is able to contribute."

> ### DEALING WITH DISAPPOINTMENT IN A RELATIONSHIP
> - Make a very detailed list of the ideal qualities and behaviors you feel the person *should* demonstrate (for example, a mother should be caring, gentle, thoughtful, interested in knowing her daughter's interests and thoughts, encouraging, and so on).
> - When the list is made, go back through it. Determine whether the person fits each quality or behavior. Mark yes or no beside each.
> - Go back through each no and pray over each one. Release your rights to having that person be the way *you* want and give each disappointment up as your love gift to Jesus.

I asked Laura to do a project that would help her to grieve her relationship with her mother (see "Dealing with Disappointment in a Relationship" above). Because I anticipated that she might feel uncomfortable being specific about all the ways her mother had disappointed her, I told her, "I know you're going to feel disloyal doing the project, but this is not meant to be criticism of your mother. It is about your coming to terms with your situation and then being able to appreciate what you have."

When Laura came back to see me the following week, she told me that she had not been able to do the project I had assigned her. I realized that she could not handle the guilt of acknowledging negative things about someone she loved. So I asked her if we could work together on compiling a list of what was negative as well as positive about her mother. She agreed, and we came up with a list that looked something like this:

Negative	Positive
She doesn't spend enough time with me.	She is generous.
She does not share herself.	She can be fun.
Her love is conditional.	When she is happy with me I know it.
She only praises my appearance.	
She isn't spiritually minded.	

After we finished making the list, I explained to Laura that she needed to pray through each negative thing, giving it to God and thanking Him for the positive things about her mother. "When you acknowledge that your mom cannot change and then release your right to the pain of your disappointments to God as a love gift, you can be free to appreciate what she can be to you. Realistic expectations pave the way for pain-free relationships.

"The question in a situation like this is not why God didn't let you have a mother who was loving and supportive in all things. The question is, what is God saying to you now? What does He want for your life? God always has something redemptive, a change for the better, in the pain of His children. This is His nature. His plan may be different from what you expect, but He means for this to bring about spiritual beauty in your life."

I assured Laura of God's promise for His people in Psalm 84:11: "No good thing does He withhold from those who walk uprightly." I emphasized that her mother's inability to meet her needs was not a punishment or the consequence of a sinful act on Laura's part. As Paul wrote, "He who did not spare His own Son, but delivered Him over for us all, how will He not also with Him freely give us all things?" (Romans 8:32). The "things" Paul is talking about are all that God has planned for His children from the beginning of the world, according to Ephesians 1:3-6.

As we talked about these passages, I said, "Because He gave His Son for you, the greatest gift in the world, He will only do what is best for you. His love for you is unconditional, and He proved it by sending Jesus to die for you. He wants to take you beyond your ideals to something better."

Laura and I met weekly for five weeks, working on her need to recognize that her value was based on far more than what she looked like. As the crisis passed and Laura came to terms with her pain regarding her mother and gained confidence in her value as God's beloved child, she asked me if we could continue meeting, but in a mentoring capacity. She said, "I want to grow in godly things. I want to be a pastor's wife and be involved in women's ministries. But I don't know how to get myself ready to be who I want to be."

I didn't want Laura to look to me to take the place of her mother. Her need for a mother was great. Her demands and expectations could have been overwhelming. This is a problem with many women who are lacking in their mother-daughter relationships. I did not want her to expect that I, or any other person, could fill that role in her life. My job as her mentor was to encourage her to mature in Christ. For her own emotional and spiritual health, Laura needed to find her satisfaction in Christ, to learn and take from many godly women without being possessive.

FROM CRISIS TO MATURITY

Whenever I anticipate a long-term mentoring relationship with a woman, I ask God to show me what her level of spiritual maturity is and to confirm whether we should continue meeting. I do not have the time or energy to mentor a large number of women. Because of this, it encourages me to remember that Jesus invested deeply in only twelve men. Even though He loved the world and touched many, His primary focus was on a small group. He was leading His disciples into spiritual maturity, preparing them to impact the world in His name.

A person's spiritual maturity actually has many components, but Psalm 116:12-17 boils it down to *four stages*.

> What shall I render to the LORD
> For all His benefits toward me?
> I shall lift up the cup of *salvation*
> And call upon the name of the LORD.
> I shall *pay my vows to the LORD*,
> Oh may it be in the presence of all His people.
> Precious in the sight of the LORD
> Is the *death of His godly ones*.
> O LORD, surely I am Your servant,

I am Your servant, the son of Your handmaid,
You have loosed my bonds.
To You I shall offer *a sacrifice of thanksgiving*,
And call upon the name of the LORD. (emphasis mine)

I use the four stages highlighted in this psalm to evaluate if and how to proceed in a mentoring relationship with someone. Let me show you how I did this with Laura.

Stage 1: Salvation—During our first counseling session, Laura clearly told me when and how she had given her heart to Jesus. I did not doubt her salvation, but I needed to know if she had moved beyond that point. At what stage was she spiritually? I needed to know if I was going to be able to help her become who God wanted her to be.

Stage 2: A desire to please God—People at this stage of spiritual maturity struggle with their self-life being in control rather than the Holy Spirit. They feel close to God when they have been to church or a conference or have enjoyed some sort of spiritual high, but that intimacy quickly fades when their desire to please God is uprooted by the temptation to please themselves. Most people at this level of spiritual maturity feel that other Christians are doing a better job of living the Christian life than they are.

Stage 3: Death to self—Paul wrote, "I have been crucified with Christ; and it is no longer I who live, but Christ lives in me; and the life which I now live in the flesh I live by faith in the Son of God, who loved me and gave Himself up for me" (Galatians 2:20). Like Paul, Christians at this stage of maturity want Christ to live out His life through them, and they give Him the control of their inner being. They give the reins of their life over to God and give up or "die" to their rights.

Death to self is not a once-and-for-all step. It is a daily, sometimes hourly, choice to place our will under God's hand. When Scripture makes references to "walking in the Spirit" (Galatians 5:16,25; Romans 8:4) or being "filled with the Spirit" (Ephesians 5:18), it simply means to be controlled by God Himself. For example, if we are controlled by anger, we will not be filled (or controlled) by the Spirit. If we want to be alive to God, we must die to self: "Consider yourselves to be dead to sin [self], but alive to God in Christ Jesus" (Romans 6:11).

Stage 4: Ability to offer a sacrifice of thanksgiving—A sacrifice of thanksgiving is an expression to God of total trust because of who we know Him to be. Believers at this final stage of spiritual maturity are able to thank God for the painful things in life that they don't understand or even like. They know that hard things come from His hand, and they rest in the truth that He's a good God who uses pain in their lives for His redemptive purposes.

Because Laura had already told me that she felt her roommate and classmates were stronger believers than she was, and because she described her spiritual life as a "roller coaster," I knew she was at a stage 2 level of spiritual maturity. I believed that she truly desired to please God, but needed help to mature beyond that point.

As she and I talked about where she was spiritually, I assured her that her feelings were a normal part of her faith development—and that we were going to work on getting her to mature into stages 3 and 4. During the years that Laura was at Multnomah Bible College, we worked on her spiritual development and on helping her learn to die to self and offer sacrifices of thanksgiving.

GETTING THERE

In mentoring Laura, I followed the biblical pattern that I believe Paul set out in 1 Corinthians:

> I do not write these things to shame you, but to *admonish* you
> as *my beloved children.* For if you were to have countless tutors

in Christ, yet you would not have many fathers, for in Christ Jesus I became your father through the gospel. Therefore I exhort you, *be imitators of me.* For this reason I have sent to you Timothy, who is my beloved and faithful child in the Lord, and he will remind you of my ways which are in Christ, just as *I teach* everywhere in every church. Now some have become arrogant, as though I were not coming to you. But *I will come to you soon*, if the Lord wills, and I shall find out, not the words of those who are arrogant but their power. For the kingdom of God does not consist in words but in power. What do you desire? Shall I *come to you with a rod*, or with love and a spirit of gentleness? (4:14-21)

Warn Her

> ". . . but to admonish you . . ."

As her spiritual mentor, whenever I saw Laura making lifestyle choices that would lead to sin and take her away from God, I had the responsibility to warn her of the consequences of going against God's Word.

One day she let me know that she had met a nice young man at work, and I asked her to tell me about him. I listened for clues as to whether he was a believer. Because Laura did not mention his walk with God, I asked her, "Where is he spiritually?" Laura was too immersed in the situation to look down the road and see the consequences of her actions, but I could, and so I sought to help her see the possible result of going out with a non-Christian.

When she said, "I think he goes to church. But I'm not going to marry him. I'll just hang out with him." I pointed out that she would not spend time with someone she was not attracted to and that eventually she would end up marrying someone she had "just hung out" with. "Laura, it is nearly impossible to control the heart once it is exposed. When the Scripture says 'do not,' we had better pay attention. Second Corinthians 6:14-15 says, 'Do not be bound together with unbelievers; for what partnership have righteousness and lawlessness, or what fellowship has light with darkness? Or what harmony has Christ with Belial, or what has a believer in common with an unbeliever?'"

Laura quickly protested, "But in our case it's different! We have a lot in common. We like the same music, we think alike and understand each other, we want to go to the same places and do the same things, we even enjoy the same food. So the Bible can't be right on that."

"Laura, I know you're not planning on it, but suppose you do end up marrying this man. When the time comes, you will have to make decisions together about where you will spend your money, your time, what you value in life, and how you will raise your children. All of those decisions will be impacted by whether you share a common faith. That will be the real test of whether there is fellowship, partnership, and commonality between you. I know that you want to please God. A relationship with this guy, if he is not walking with God, is wrong."

Because I wanted Laura to move beyond the level of wanting to please God, I challenged her to fall in love with Jesus and assigned her a project to help her learn how (see "Falling in Love with Jesus" below).

FALLING IN LOVE WITH JESUS

Do a word study on *love*. Use a separate concordance or the one in the back of your Bible. To do a word study:

- Make a list of all the verses on love, writing out the key phrase in each one.
- Make the statements about God's love your own by rewriting the verses with your name in them. As you personalize them, remind yourself that these verses are God's love letters to you.
- Answer these questions: If what God says about me in the Bible is true and I believe it, what difference can that make in my life? How can I live in light of that truth every day?

Love Her

> ". . . my beloved children . . ."

I loved Laura by showing her unconditional love and acceptance. I did this by exercising patience while she was growing at her pace, not mine. By being understanding and listening to her patiently while she shared, I showed her that I didn't expect her to grow up overnight. I also chose to believe the best of her and reflected that to her whenever possible. The Bible tells us that without love we are nothing (see 1 Corinthians 13:2), and I was conscious of that in the mentoring process. I always gave Laura a welcome hug and a good-bye squeeze. It was not hard to love Laura, and my love for her deepened as I prayed for her and asked for God's blessing on her life and her struggles.

Model Consistent Christlikeness

> ". . . imitators of me . . ."

As Laura's mentor I was called to be an example to her. My words would make no difference if I did not live out and validate them with my actions and lifestyle. Paul looked daily to the Lord, and he could say that his ways were "in Christ." I didn't feel worthy of setting an example for Laura or anybody else, but "Christ in me" did, and I could look to Him to teach and guide me. God does not ask perfection of me; He asks for a consistent, godly life, one that faithfully acknowledges my dependence on Him and admits my frailties to others, including those I mentor.

After Laura and I had been meeting for a while and I knew that I could trust her not to drain me or monopolize my time, I occasionally invited her to our home. I wanted her to observe a different family dynamic than the one she had grown up with. Sometimes I took her along to a conference or a meeting where I was speaking. I carefully chose the events that I invited her to because I didn't want her to be uncomfortable when I had to leave her on her own while I ministered to other women. She needed to learn, without having to be with me constantly. There were times when I chose not to take her because it would be exhausting for me. I sought to be consistent with the boundaries God had shown me. I tried to show Laura an everyday Christianity through being authentic as I drove, talked on the phone, prayed, spoke to others, and so on.

Look for Opportunities to Teach Her About God

". . . I teach . . ."

I sought to teach Laura about God in a variety of ways: through example, informal conversation, and regular Bible study on a subject that she wanted to grow in. Sometimes I had her turn to a passage in the Bible that addressed something she was facing and asked her to read it out loud to me. Then we discussed what she believed the passage was saying about her circumstances.

As her mentor I was responsible to bring the truth of the Word of God into our times together, to help her grow up in Christ, be more like Him, know Him better, and fall in love with Him.

Be Supportive

" . . . I will come to you soon . . ."

Paul's promise to the Corinthians that he would come soon showed his desire to be with them. It was an enormous affirmation of the Corinthian church. I wanted to affirm Laura by believing in her, standing by her, and sticking up for her because of her huge need for approval. So when Laura shared a particularly clear spiritual insight, I let her see my appreciation of her sensitivity. As I got to know her better, I pointed out strengths that I saw in her and encouraged her to use them in other areas of her life. For example, there were times when she had to confront a roommate about a conflict they were having. She always expressed concern about whether she could face it. Having gone through several similar situations with her, I was able to remind her of God's faithfulness to her in the past and of how well she had managed herself.

One day I was sitting in the cafeteria and I overheard some young women discussing Laura and her beauty. I leaned over and said, "If you think she's beautiful on the outside, you should get to know her. Laura loves God and wants to please Him in every area of her life. She would make a wonderful friend." As Laura's mentor, I had the responsibility to represent her well before others.

Hold Her Accountable

" . . . I come to you with a rod . . ."

One day, a week before graduation, Laura walked into my office very upset. As soon as I asked her what was wrong, she confessed that she had cheated on two of her finals. As we talked, I reminded her that when she got under pressure it was easy to revert to her old ways. I sensed that she had cheated out of a desire to be successful in her mother's eyes.

"What do you think I should do?" she wailed.

"What is more important is what *you* think you should do," I responded.

"If I confess what I've done to my professors, they might not let me graduate. My family has already bought the plane tickets and they will lose all that money! How can I tell them? And what will my friends think? I will be disgraced, and my mother will be disappointed with me!

"If you graduate and walk out of this school experience without confessing what you have done, I fear that God's blessing will be off your life," I replied. It was not easy for me to be so strong, but it was the truth. Holding Laura accountable to do the hard thing was my way of using the rod. I reminded her of the blessing that God promises for obedience:

"Oh that they had such a heart in them, that they would fear Me and keep all My commandments always, that it may be well with them and with their sons forever!" (Deuteronomy 5:29).

Laura and I reviewed the principles of death to self. I said, "Remember how you gave up your rights to your mother's approval when we first started meeting? I think you need to go back to that principle. Love gifts are an outworking of death to self. We give Him a love gift when we give Him anything in our life that is not pleasing to Him, anything that comes between Him and us. We choose to do it because we love Jesus more than self."

Laura replied, "I want to please God, and my relationship with Him is more important than what my mother or professors think. I have to go and confess."

I was crying with her when I said, "You go right now. I won't see another person until I hear from you. I will stay here and pray for you. When you are done, come back and tell me what you did."

After we prayed together, Laura went off in fear and trembling to find her professors. When she returned, she sank gratefully into the big chair in my office and told me they were going to let her graduate because of her honesty. But, because the professors believed in consequences, Laura was required to do special projects to make up for the exam grades. It wasn't easy, but Laura knew that by doing the right thing she could honor God and be unashamed.

Moving Her On

Throughout the time I met with Laura, I prayed about how God would have me help not only in her problems, but also in the bigger picture of her life. I believe He put her in my life to help her to better understand who she is in His eyes, where she stands with Him, and who He made her to be. As her mentor I wanted to nurture her to spiritual maturity.

As I look at Laura's life since graduation, I see that she passed those tests to her faith. She allowed God to use her challenges to strengthen her Christian character. Today I see her making right choices, and she has been blessed because of it. She chose to marry a man who is successful in the secular world and strong in the Lord. Both have a strong Christian witness with their neighbors and associates. Laura has stayed faithful to God and is a woman of influence in her church.

PART 2:

help for
dealing
with
specific
issues

anger

WHAT YOU NEED TO KNOW

Anger, a strong emotion that inflames and enrages the one who feels it, is normally a secondary response to other emotions, such as frustration, helplessness, and fear. Just as pain can signal an illness, so anger can be a symptom of an unhealed hurt. While anger can be appropriate and godly—as was Jesus' anger at the moneychangers in the temple or at the hypocrisy of the Pharisees—our anger can be destructive if we do not deal with it appropriately.

Following is a list of some common causes of anger.

- *A real or perceived physical or emotional threat* that evokes a need to protect one's self or a loved one. I know a mother who is afraid that her son is making unwise choices; but instead of talking with him about her fear, she expresses it by being angry with him.
- *An unforgiving spirit.* Anger can come from unresolved problems or hurts that have caused resentment. An elderly widow

once told me that she was furious with her dead husband. After his death, she had realized that for most of her married life she had repressed who she was in order to live peacefully with him. At the core of her anger was the need to forgive herself and her husband.

- *A lack of rest or alone time, extreme dieting, lack of exercise, or sustained pressure or stress.* Each of these can deplete the body's energy reserves. When this happens, things that normally do not bother a woman can upset her. In such cases, anger is the body's way of signaling a need for self-preservation.

- *Unacknowledged anger at God.* Few Christians are willing to admit they are angry with God. They know that God could change or "fix" their situation, and if He doesn't, they blame Him. However, because they feel it is wrong to be angry with God, they project their frustration about Him onto the people who are closest to them.

- *An unchangeable situation.* For instance, many women experience deep anger at parents who are incapable of giving them affection. Confronting someone who is unable to change will not help the situation and will most likely aggravate it.

Most people deal with anger in one of two ways:

1. *Repression/denial*—Many Christians realize that unresolved anger is destructive and therefore sinful. But because they don't know what to do with their angry feelings, some simply *decide* that they are not angry. Their anger (which does not go away) gets buried in their subconscious, but eventually breaks out in other forms, such as depression, meanness, slander, withholding affection, and other ugly manifestations. These forms of repressed anger hurt everyone—both the bearer and the receiver. Repression and denial are unhealthy and not God's way. If a counselee continues to be in denial about her anger, a KTC cannot help her.

2. *Inappropriate expression*—Our culture often encourages us to express our anger by acting out what we feel. This could include blowing up, being sarcastic or impatient, telling people off, throwing things, yelling, hitting, kicking, slamming fists through walls, and so on. Such expressions of anger hurt everyone and everything in their path and do not honor God.

When you are working with a woman who has unresolved anger issues, keep in mind that it usually takes time to identify the source of anger and then to process it. Les Carter and Frank Minirth's book *The Anger Workbook: A Thirteen Step Interactive Plan to Help You* is helpful when working with women who have anger issues.

HELP AND HOPE FROM GOD'S WORD

Spend time reading and meditating on the following passages of Scripture, asking God to show you how you can use them to help someone who struggles with this issue.

Psalm 37:8
Proverbs 14:17; 16:32; 19:11
Ecclesiastes 7:9
Ephesians 4:26
Colossians 3:8-10
James 1:19-20

LANCE THE BOIL

When Cynthia asked to talk with me, she said, "I don't know what is wrong with me. I am upset with my children. I am screaming and jerking them around. I realize they are just being kids, but I am so angry. Please help me understand what is going on."

To get to the bottom of her problem, I needed to help Cynthia find the root or reason for her anger. When we met together, I asked her to describe her feelings and to tell me why she thought her children made her angry all the time. As she talked, I asked her some questions to help her identify her anger triggers:

- Is the situation that arouses your anger a normal one? For example, do you get angry at your teen for not behaving like an adult?
- Were you angry because you felt out of control?
- Can you change the circumstances that make you angry?
- Are you angry about sin in your life or someone else's?
- Is this appropriate or reasonable anger? (Some anger is motivated by selfishness and is therefore inappropriate. However, there are times when it is an acceptable or normal response.)

One question in particular was significant: Is there a pattern here? In other words, do you get angry when the same thing happens repeatedly? In answering this, Cynthia told me that she found herself unreasonably angry when her husband was traveling. His absences had increased in recent months and so had her anger. She also said that she was more upset after phone conversations with her parents.

Cynthia felt guilty about her angry outbursts at her children. She knew if these continued that she could damage her kids, but she didn't know the cause of her anger. Cynthia's answers showed me that the anger at her children was actually a symptom of something deeper. As we talked, it became clear that she had several areas of woundedness that were at the root of her angry feelings. I sensed that she needed to deal with some abandonment issues and that we would need to look more closely at her growing-up years and her life in general.

MEET HER FELT NEED

In order to come alongside of Cynthia, I said, "For years I repressed angry feelings because I felt they were sinful. But I found that they would show up in other ways, either directed at people or as frustration or irritation in odd situations." I told Cynthia how freeing it was when I saw that Ephesians 4:26 said I could be angry and not sin. It was a relief to realize that it was all right to be angry. The major issue was not my anger, but how I handled it. Anger can be a wake-up call to alert us to something that we need to work on.

I explained that I had to learn not to repress or wrongly express what I was feeling, but to *confess* to myself that I was angry. I had to own my anger by acknowledging it and admitting it to myself. Then I could confess it to God. Acknowledging my anger helped me ask for God's help, deal with the issues at the root of my emotions, and find godly ways to relieve my feelings.

I told Cynthia that I believed her anger was a symptom of some unfinished business in her life, such as buried resentments and unforgiveness, and that I wanted her to do a project before our next meeting that would help her identify those areas (see "Identifying Unhealed Hurts" below).

IDENTIFYING UNHEALED HURTS

Human beings are naturally bent toward survival and self-protection, which is why we often repress or put away painful things from our consciousness. While repression helps us keep going, it leaves us unaware of what has wounded our spirits. In order for our wounds to heal, we need to identify and acknowledge them. Here are some ways to help identify unhealed hurts:

1. Separate your life into sections according to the following stages:
   a. Conception to kindergarten (There is ample evidence to suggest that unborn children sense and feel what the mother experiences while carrying them. In the womb a child can take on a sense of rejection, particularly if the mother contemplated an abortion or struggled with wanting the pregnancy. What are your feelings about your conception?):
   b. Kindergarten through grade school:

---

c. Middle school/junior high:

d. High school:

e. College/work:

f. Career:

g. Major moves (divide into cities or employment):

h. Marriage:

i. Others (such as divorce or widowhood):

For each stage, ask yourself if there is any event or relationship that comes to mind that still has power to evoke a negative response. In other words, does remembering a specific incident or person make you feel like crying? Does it make you angry? Does the event or relationship cause you to feel sad, or diminished? Does it make you feel rejected, misunderstood, unloved? It could be an incident or a person, or both, that has wounded you.

2. Write down only those persons or events that still have power over you to evoke a response. If you remember something painful but it does not bring an adverse or emotional reaction, that means that you have already taken care of it or that God hasn't fingered it yet. You do not have to deal with something unless the Holy Spirit points it out to you.

3. Write down the incidents and people that come to mind for each stage, and how you felt about them. How you felt is as important as what actually happened. It may be that, looking back, you intellectually *understand* what happened. However, it is critical that you deal with what you *felt* about it at the time, because your emotions were a part of your reality.

As you reflect on each of these stages, address the following questions:

a. How did I feel about my education?

b. What about my friends?

c. What was my relationship to my siblings, my parents?

d. What were the highlights and/or lowlights of this period?

e. What were my surroundings and how did I feel about them?

4. After each stage, go through the four steps to forgiveness for each situation (see chapter 4). It may take several days. No matter how long it takes, go over each incident that you have noted and walk it through the steps to healing.

Then I said, "In the meantime, while you are working on identifying the root problem, the Holy Spirit can help you live out Colossians 3:8-10, which says to put aside anger. I believe this means that until you can fully deal with your anger, you can *choose* not to allow it to rule you. James 1:19-20 says, 'But everyone must be quick to hear, slow to speak and slow to anger; for the anger of man does not achieve the righteousness of God.' There is a call here to a change of behavior in order to bring about what God wants." We prayed together before she left and set up a time to meet again, after she had completed the project.

When we met for the second time, I asked Cynthia to talk about each hurtful incident she had identified when she did the assigned project. As she did, it became clear to both of us that her anger at her children was misdirected. She felt out of control when they misbehaved, just as she had felt when she was a child and had no control over her parents leaving her all the time. Her husband's frequent trips were also triggering her repressed anger toward her parents, and her only outlet was to yell at her kids. Cynthia felt overwhelmed as she cared for them alone. I assured her that she could take authority over her children. I told her that because she was the adult, she must put her foot down when the children misbehaved, define acceptable limits of behavior, and follow through with consequences for disobedience.

I talked to her about forgiving her husband for the times in the past when she felt he had abandoned her by leaving and counseled her to speak to him about how she felt. They needed to face her problem together and begin with a clean slate, coming up with ideas for a new way to approach his travel.

TAKE HER TO JESUS

Because Cynthia had identified the issue of her parents leaving her as an unhealed hurt, we turned to her relationship with them. I said, "Cynthia, as painful as it was for you, God knew when He put you in this family that your parents would often leave you. They will have to give account to Him for their actions, but I want you to understand it was God's plan for you to be born into your family. Whether you understand it or not, He never makes a mistake. His purpose was not to wound you." I asked Cynthia to look back and tell me what she had learned through those painful times. I did this to help her see that there could be value in the painful things she had suffered as a child.

I went on to say, "God was with you through your entire upbringing. You may not have felt His presence all of the time, but can you recall a specific time when you did?" I asked Cynthia that question because I wanted her to try to identify the times when she felt that God was with her, to underline to her that He had not abandoned her.

I took Cynthia to 2 Samuel 22:29-33 to emphasize that God's way is always perfect.

> You are my lamp, O Lord; the Lord turns my darkness into light. With your help I can advance against a troop; with my God I can scale a wall. As for God, *his way is perfect;* the word of the Lord is flawless. He is a shield for all who take refuge in him. For who is God besides the Lord? And who is the Rock except our God? It is God who arms me with strength and *makes my way perfect* (NIV, emphasis mine).

In these verses David reminded himself of who God is. He asserted that because God is perfect, He cannot make a mistake. When he wrote those words, David was struggling. He was running from his enemies and felt he was in an impossible situation. That's how Cynthia was feeling. She was one person standing against many impossibilities. She sometimes felt as if she had hit a brick wall and couldn't get around it, avoid it, or go through it. I wanted to show her that she could say with David, "By my God I can leap over it!" I said to her, "Healing from the pain of your past will not always feel good, but God is with you. He will help you forgive your parents."

I assured her that she could follow David's example of remembering *who* God is. I asked her, "Is God your rock? Is He your fortress? Is God's Word true? Who will you rest in? Your husband, your abilities, your talents? God is the only One who can make your way perfect."

I reminded her that she was not alone in the process of overcoming the wounds from her past; God is always with us. The things that made her the angriest could be instruments in His hand to bring about good in her life, if she would let Him.

After we had explored the negative and positive sides of her childhood traumas, I felt Cynthia was ready to move on to forgiveness. I talked with her about the principles of forgiveness and I explained the concept of giving God love gifts. A love gift is something we are doing or thinking that we give God because we know it does not please Him. A love gift, then, can be anything that could come between God and us that we have turned over to Him. It is a daily — sometimes hourly — choice to place our will under God's hand. In Cynthia's case, giving God her right to be angry with her parents would be a love gift to Him. When the Scriptures speak of "walking in the Spirit" (Galatians 5:16,25), it means to be controlled by God Himself. If we are controlled by anger, or anything else, the Spirit will not control us.

HELP HER BECOME INDEPENDENTLY DEPENDENT

Once Cynthia had done the work of forgiveness and was daily making the choice to give God her right to be angry, I knew she was on her way to wholeness. I told her that we no longer needed to meet regularly, but that I would be available if she hit another crisis or wanted to talk something over.

During our last meeting I gave her an exercise that she could do whenever she felt that she was facing an impossible situation (see "Hot Pen Journaling" on page 104). I told her, "Journaling can help pinpoint what you are feeling and why. When we are yielded and looking to God, our difficulties can become an opportunity through which He can show us Himself. Part of His character is that He is the God of the impossible: The things impossible with men are possible with God." (See Matthew 19:26.)

HOT PEN JOURNALING

When you are in turmoil, get a blank sheet of paper and ask yourself, "What could be disturbing me?" Write everything that comes to mind. Allow it to come right off the top of your head. Bring up everything that you can possibly think of that could be bothering you.

This exercise is the mental equivalent of cleaning out a desk drawer. A drawer can get so full that you don't really know what is there until you pull it all out and put everything in it on the table.

As you write, don't try to make anything connect. Don't bother to sweeten it or worry about the spelling. Pull it out of your heart, put it down, and go on. When nothing more comes to mind, read through what you have written, asking God to reveal what is going on in your heart. Most of the time you will be able to see a theme that runs through what you have written. The real issue could be lack of trust, jealousy, fear of aging, lack of forgiveness, and so on. Once the root has been identified, you can deal with the core issue by asking God and others for forgiveness and using the Word of God to guide you in godly attitudes.

Cynthia had learned that she needed to continually speak the truth about her feelings. After our times together, she realized that her husband was often oblivious to her needs. She saw that it was her responsibility to talk to him in a loving way so that her resentment would not grow. It took time for her to learn to do this, but she developed a conviction about it because of what she had learned from God's Word.

When she learned how to control her own emotions, Cynthia was able to bring discipline and control into her family. After forgiving her parents, she began to view them in a different light and learned to enjoy them as people who cared for her, not as parents who let her down.

controlling husbands

WHAT YOU NEED TO KNOW

A husband who is controlling his family is actually subjecting them to a form of abuse. Some controlling husbands are that way because their fathers were. Others wrongly believe that the Bible gives them permission to control when it says that the husband is to be the head of the home (see Ephesians 5:22; 1 Corinthians 11:3).

Family abuse involves a variety of behaviors that result in the wounding of the souls of the children and spouse. Emotional abuse is trying to control family members through manipulation of their emotions, sense of worth, and safety.[1] *Passive emotional abuse* includes words and actions that disregard, ignore, or downplay the abilities of a person. *Active emotional abuse* includes berating, name calling, and verbal harassment in order to control.[2]

Many families are made up of hurting people. Steve Earll, a licensed professional counselor says,

Recognizing that there will be troubled families does not excuse the abuse and neglect that often occurs. Instead, facing the reality of traumatic situations allows an individual to work through the issues, grieve the trauma, and move into healing. . . . Trauma that is unresolved does not get stored away in a secret compartment never to return. Instead it acts as an acid that seeps into and poisons every aspect of our lives, clouding our ability to deal with new trauma and enjoy the good aspects of life.[3]

An excellent book that can be helpful when counseling women with controlling husbands is *Boundaries in Marriage* by Dr. Henry Cloud and Dr. John Townsend.

HELP AND HOPE FROM GOD'S WORD

Spend time reading and meditating on the following passages of Scripture, asking God to show you how you can use them to help someone who struggles with this issue.

Deuteronomy 31:6
1 Chronicles 28:9
Nehemiah 8:10
Mark 11:15-17
2 Corinthians 6:16
Philippians 4:8-9
1 John 3:1

LANCE THE BOIL

Cindy, who had been married for ten years, came to see me because she was having difficulty in her marriage. She said, "One of the things that attracted me to my husband was that he was always sure of himself and knew what he thought. I saw myself as a fragile flower and him as an oak tree. But what I was drawn to when we were dating has become a problem in our marriage. He is so sure of what he thinks about everything that he won't listen to me. If I disagree with him, he gets angry. When it was just the two of us, I learned to keep quiet and do things his way, but now we have three children to disagree over. He is always mad at me or the children. All of us tiptoe around, trying not to upset him. I love him, but I don't like him at all, nor do I like the person I have become in this marriage. There doesn't seem to be any way out."

I had known Cindy since she was in high school. The woman sitting in front of me was not the vibrant, exuberant girl I had grown to love. Her demeanor was sad and shrinking. Because of this I asked her, "Is he hurting you or the children physically?" I had to know, because if physical abuse was part of the equation, my counsel to her would have been very different.

Cindy answered, "No, not to this point, but he gets so upset that I wouldn't be surprised if he did hit me or the kids."

"Have you talked to him about this? Have you told him what you feel and what you fear?"

"No," she answered, "I am afraid I will make him more angry. I learned to keep quiet before the kids came and that seems to be the only way I can cope."

"Cindy, you have to stop the cycle of your husband's treatment of you and the children. By remaining silent, you play into what he is doing and you actually encourage him to continue."

TAKE HER TO JESUS

Second Corinthians 6:16 and other passages tell us that the believer is the temple of the Holy Spirit of God. In Mark 11:15-17, Jesus set the example of how the temple should be treated. When He found the moneychangers breaking the law of God by being there, He put a stop to it. They had gone too far! I believe that a woman can draw the line like Jesus did and say, "I am God's temple; you can go no further."

This is a delicate line because many women do not seek God's face and instead use their own criteria for what violates them as God's temple. I wanted to help Cindy understand that her husband's angry treatment of her was a violation of Christ in her. By speaking out, she could choose to break the cycle of mistreatment. She could place her life and identity in God's hands and choose to walk in His strength.

Many women in this situation are afraid of their husbands and resist making any changes that may rock the boat. I wanted Cindy to develop a conviction based on God's Word that confronting her husband's mistreatment was a matter of obedience, so I told her, "It will not be easy and you will probably be frightened. It will require courage and grace, which God promises to give you. Deuteronomy 31:6 says, 'Be strong and courageous, do not be afraid or tremble at them, for the LORD your God is the one who goes with you. He will not fail you or forsake you.' You will have Him with you when you speak to your husband. Let's talk about how you can approach him."

Paul told the Ephesians, "Speaking the truth in love, we are to grow up in all aspects into Him who is the head, even Christ" (Ephesians 4:15). That means that speaking the truth in a kind, loving way is showing spiritual maturity. A wife with a controlling husband needs to speak to him about his wrongful behavior. Paul continued, "Therefore, laying aside falsehood, SPEAK TRUTH EACH ONE OF YOU WITH HIS NEIGHBOR, for we are members of one another" (verse 25). A woman's husband is her closest neighbor. And finally, "BE ANGRY AND YET DO NOT SIN; do not let the sun go down on your anger, and do not give the devil an opportunity" (verses 26-27). That means that today's problem must be settled today or we give the Devil an opening. What will the Devil do? He will come between a wife and her husband. When we hide the truth, Satan uses the opportunity to beat us into such a state that self-pity can take root.

I told Cindy, "You can make a new determination to do as God says and speak the truth to your husband. If you are ready to do that, it would be best to start with prayer, confessing that, up until now, you haven't done it God's way. Ask God to forgive you and give you strength to speak up."

After we prayed, I reminded Cindy that when she obeys God, He will be there with her to hold her hand when she confronts her husband. "Now walk with dignity before him. As a daughter of the King, you can say, 'From now on I will not let you speak to me that way.'"

Cindy was relieved after we prayed. She knew that the hard part would be when she faced her husband, and she was concerned about what was sure to arise in the coming weeks. I said, "Take baby steps with your confronting. Slowly begin to let him know that things must change between you."

Cindy and I discussed ways that she could speak to her husband about the cycle of behavior they had each fallen into. I told her that a rule of thumb in confrontation needs to be heavy on the *I* and light on the *you*. After much prayer we decided that she should say something like this: "I want to talk to you about a pattern that we have in our marriage that I think is becoming destructive to our family and our relationship. When you become angry with me or the children, I get very frightened. It has gotten to the point where I feel I cannot say anything that is different from what you think. I have not spoken to you about it and I am sorry. I should have been more faithful to say how I feel. I love you and want to work this out. But things have to change." I told her that if he were to become so angry that he attempted to physically hurt her, she was to take the children and get away from him until they could work it out with a godly mediator.

As she talked, it became clear to me that her husband's control in their marriage was a true problem. But she also had allowed herself to fall into self-pity. Yes, her marriage was not easy, but Cindy was unconsciously relieving her choked emotions by talking about it to others. This is a trap that many women fall into (see "The Self-Pity Trap" below).

THE SELF-PITY TRAP

Many women facing troubles fall into the trap of self-pity, which is sometimes a way for a hurting person to get attention and gain sympathy. Self-pity is self-absorption and self-centeredness. I believe that self-pity originates in the mind, where thoughts, perceptions, and feelings are born. Most self-pity begins with a real problem and spirals down into a "poor me" attitude. Because they may think it is more spiritual to be quiet than to confront and speak truth, some women do not realize that they are stuck in self-pity.

If our focus is on the heartaches and disappointments we have faced, we will naturally feel sorry for ourselves. What we center our thoughts on will determine our actions and our attitude.

The KTC can encourage the one wallowing in self-pity to choose to focus on all the lovely things in her life and lay aside self-pity. Philippians 4:8-9 gives us specifics about where our focus should be. It also tells us what the result of that new perspective will be: the presence of the God of peace.

When a woman recognizes that she is in the trap of self-pity, she can allow God to turn her difficult situation into something He can use to bless others. I have seen God put iron in the blood of some women who formerly wallowed in self-absorption and self-centeredness.

I pointed out that her own attitude and thinking needed to change and asked her to read 1 Chronicles 28:9: "Serve Him with a whole heart and a willing mind; for the LORD searches all hearts, and understands every intent of the thoughts." I said, "If this is true about God, we dare not be careless with our hearts and thoughts. What you think about yourself and your value comes out in your behavior, whether you want it to or not." I asked her to do the project that would help her monitor her self-talk (see "Monitoring Self-Talk" on page 111) when she got home, so that she could get a better idea of what she was saying to herself. I knew that she was probably saying things to herself that she didn't even realize. Cindy had suppressed her feelings for so long in order to keep the peace that she had lost confidence in herself and what she knew to be right. She was tearing herself down even more with her self-talk.

> ### MONITORING SELF-TALK
>
> Ask yourself the following questions[4] every time you notice that you are feeling depressed. Write down your answers so you can go over them with someone.
>
> - What am I saying to myself that is making me feel this way?
> - Am I telling the truth, or am I talking to myself about what I am afraid of and believing it to be true?
> - Am I holding myself to a standard of perfection that is impossible?
> - Do I ever say, "I must. . ." or "I should . . ."? When does that happen?
> - Do I *want* to feel this way? (Some people thrive on being upset because there is no other excitement in their lives. Many live from crisis to crisis until they can live no other way.)

I reflected back to her what she had revealed to me of her thoughts about herself: "I have heard you say, 'if only I were not afraid to say what I think, if I were prettier, if I were skinnier, if I were a better housekeeper, if my children were better behaved, then my husband would be nicer to me and maybe things would be different in our marriage.' Things are not the way you wish and if you live with an 'if only' state of mind and heart, you will not find God's perspective or way for your life. It will breed discontent and cancel out the joy of the Lord."

I was concerned that Cindy was spending a lot of energy worrying about what might happen in the future if her husband didn't change, so I told her, "Those kinds of thoughts can lead to more discouragement and depression. Have you noticed that kind of thinking usually comes when it is dark, or when you are exhausted or cannot sleep at night? Those 'what ifs' can come even after things have gone well between you and your husband. That is the Enemy trying to take advantage of your fatigue. You must reject those fears in Jesus' name and take a stand against Satan."

Nehemiah said to the people, "Do not be grieved, for the joy of the LORD is your strength" (8:10). In Nehemiah's time God's people were grieving over their past sins and losses. God called them not to mourn anymore. He gave the Jews strength to face the truth and grace to change

> **THANKFULNESS**
> - Take a blank sheet of paper.
> - Fill it with a list of all the things you can be thankful for. Ask yourself what you have that others might not, such as sheets to sleep on, food to eat, hot water, electricity. Notice things that you may take for granted that people in other places may not enjoy.
> - Pray through the list, expressing thanks to God for each item on it.

what needed to be changed. "That is God's promise to you, Cindy," I said. "Let's look at what is true about your circumstances." I had Cindy tell me some good things about her husband and her marriage. We talked about ways she could encourage those characteristics in her husband and focus on them. I assured her that God's plan for their life together was that they enjoy one another and that she respect her husband.

I asked her if she would be willing to do a project that could help her become more thankful (see "Thankfulness" to the left) in addition to the self-talk project before our next visit. My prayer was that she would be challenged to face what she might be saying to herself that could contribute to the negative cycle in her marriage and that, at the same time, she would come to grips with the many things she could be thankful for.

BELIEVE FOR HER

Cindy made an appointment to see me in a week. I asked her to report to me how she had acted on God's Word in confronting her husband. I shared how precious God's presence would be when she had been faithful in obedience to Him. I said, "Our Lord will show His love to you. First John 3:1 says that His love is lavished on you."

Because Cindy's tender heart had been squashed by a controlling husband, she had come to think that the negative things she said to herself were true. I believed for her by reflecting to her how Christ saw her and by calling her attention to the untrue things she said about herself. I promised to do that until she could believe it for herself. I said to her,

"You may not feel it, Cindy, but you are precious to God. You are His treasure."

HELP HER BECOME INDEPENDENTLY DEPENDENT

Cindy came to see me regularly for four months. We talked about what happened each week between her and her husband. I encouraged Cindy when she had wisely confronted her husband. There were times when I helped her plan how to speak to him about something he had said or done to her or the children. I had to continually remind her of her value and worth in God's eyes as she stepped out bravely to confront her husband, going against the pattern of behavior that she had followed for many years.

One day she came and said, "I got sick and tired of being so careful about everything I say, so this week I let myself say exactly what I was thinking to my husband. It surprised me that I could speak so strongly. But I learned a sad lesson. Because I did not choose my words, he responded to me like he used to and I could feel the fear welling back up inside me."

As Cindy grew more able to recognize when she needed to put a stop to her husband's controlling behavior and how to speak to him, she made fewer and fewer appointments with me. Now occasionally she will call to process a particularly challenging situation. A few months ago she said, "I have learned so much about healthy confronting and establishing boundaries. The amazing thing is that, as I have learned to love my husband by speaking truth to him, my confidence in myself and my commitment to our marriage has grown."

depression and burnout

WHAT YOU NEED TO KNOW

Caution: Encourage your counselee to see a professional if she exhibits more than one of the following signs for longer than two weeks. Severe depression is most likely the cause if five or more of the following symptoms have been present during the same two-week period and represent a change from previous functioning:

- depression, feeling of sadness
- diminished interest or pleasure in activities
- change in appetite, significant weight loss without dieting, or weight gain (for example, a change of more than 5 percent of body weight in a month)
- insomnia or hypersomnia
- fatigue/energy losses
- feelings of worthlessness or excessive/inappropriate guilt
- diminished ability to think or concentrate
- recurrent thoughts of death, suicide

Severe depression, though not uncommon, is not as prevalent as low-grade depression. When you meet with a woman who has a low-grade depression, ask her:

- *About her health.* Her discouragement may be the result of an infection or an illness. If you think she is ill, have her see a doctor and report back to you.
- *About her sleep patterns, and discern if she is getting enough rest.* If fatigue is the problem, work with her on a plan to cut back on her schedule in order to get some sleep and recuperate. On the other hand, sleeping more than normal may also be a sign of emotional difficulties.
- *What she does to relax and rejuvenate.* A low-grade depression can be the result of all work and no play. She may simply need to play more—to see a movie with her husband or a friend, to spend a day at the beach, or to go on a shopping trip or on an excursion with friends.
- *About her eating.* Is she dieting excessively, overeating, or having too much sugar or an unbalanced diet? Depression can be the result of an irregular diet. If from her response you feel that her eating is part of the problem, help her make a plan for how she can bring that into balance. Work with her on a simple meal plan, including three meals a day. Address her need for protein, carbohydrates, fruits, and vegetables. If she is concerned about weight gain, encourage her to eat wisely and in small amounts.
- *Whether she is getting regular exercise.* Regular exercise is a simple way to combat low-grade depression. With exercise, the body releases endorphins that trigger a sense of well-being. If she is not getting any exercise, suggest she begin by taking a brisk ten-minute walk or run when she feels particularly

sad. If it is not convenient to exercise at that specific time, ask her to commit to making herself take that walk sometime each day. Encourage her to slowly increase the time of exercise until she is exercising for thirty minutes each day.

- *If she has recently suffered a loss of some kind:* a relationship, a job, a move or job change, even her youth. (To find out how to help her with loss, see chapter 13). Losses and the pain of them are important to acknowledge.

- *If she has encouragement and support.* Does she go to a church or a support group? What is she reading? Is she watching too much television (which can be a sign of escape from reality)? Has she withdrawn from others? People need social interaction for a sense of well-being. Work with her to decide what she can do to meet the need for interaction with others without becoming overwhelmed.

- *What she is saying to herself.* Her self-talk may be feeding her emotions. Assign her the "Monitoring Self-Talk" project on page 111. Her answers will help you determine in what direction to go.

> ### SYMPTOMS OF LOW-GRADE DEPRESSION
>
> A low-grade depression can include one or more of the following and does not last more than two weeks:
>
> - a feeling of sadness
> - exhaustion and low energy for no reason
> - feeling overwhelmed by the smallest task
> - anxiety
> - avoiding people
> - fear of being left alone
> - mental confusion
> - feeling like a failure
> - guilt
> - feeling that life is not worth living
> - hopelessness
> - no sense of future
> - irritable or angry more than usual
> - no confidence
> - feeling that life is unfair

If your counselee does not show signs of improvement or continues to deteriorate, she needs professional help.

HELP AND HOPE FROM GOD'S WORD

Spend time reading and meditating on the following passages of Scripture, asking God to show you how you can use them to help someone who struggles with this issue.

1 Kings 18–19

Psalm 56:8

Isaiah 43:2

Jeremiah 29:4-14

2 Corinthians 9:8

2 Peter 2:19

LANCE THE BOIL

My heart went out to Janet when she called me one evening and said, "Muriel, I am at the end of myself. I am crying all the time and am not coping very well with life. Every time the doorbell or phone rings I think, *I can't take any more*, and I can barely get up in the morning. I don't know what is wrong with me. If I can get a plane ticket, can I come and see you? I need help to figure out how to deal with this."

Janet, whom I had watched grow up, was like a daughter to me. I told her to come as soon as she could. She arranged child care for her two kids and flew out on the first flight available. I picked her up at the airport, drove her to our house, put her in a comfortable chair, and gave her a cup of hot tea.

"Tell me everything that's going on in your life," I said when we had settled in. As Janet talked and cried for hours, clues to her depressed state slowly came to light. She was feeling overwhelmed, and understandably so. Her younger child was a handful, challenging Janet's authority on every hand. Janet was exhausted from trying to hold the line with her daughter while taking care of her son as well. Her phone rang constantly with people wanting to talk, cry, or ask a favor. Her husband was a busy man, and she felt pressure to entertain his business associates, which meant keeping an extra-clean house, cooking fancy meals, and trying to please everyone.

In the previous months, Janet had also experienced a number of losses. Her parents had retired and moved many hours away to a warmer climate. Their move meant she no longer had reliable, free child care, nor did she have easy access to a large component of her emotional support. In addition, one of her close friends had recently died of breast cancer and another friend's child had been hit and killed by a drunk driver.

TAKE HER TO JESUS

Janet needed to know that she wasn't crazy. Because she could not cope with meeting her standards for herself, she was afraid that she was letting God down. She thought she was unspiritual because she had failed to manage everything well.

After Janet had talked out everything she could think of that was weighing on her heart, I helped her make a list of the things she had told me. When we finished I said, "Janet, no wonder you are struggling. Anyone with this kind of load would be depressed. Have you seen a doctor?"

"Yes, and he tells me that I should go on antidepressants, but I don't want to. Somehow it makes me seem weak and even more unspiritual; because I am a Christian I should be able to manage this."

"I used to believe that myself," I said. "Your loss of joy in things that used to bring you pleasure is a sign of depression and burnout. I learned this when I was pregnant with our second child. Shelly was three years old and I was studying Chinese at the language school in Taiwan and running a guesthouse for our mission. Things built up, and five months after Milei was born, I was in the middle of burnout, although I didn't realize it.

"My symptoms came on suddenly and started with a panic attack. I was in a crowd of people and felt I couldn't breathe. It was as if someone had closed off part of my windpipe and my mind and body felt like they were suffocating. When I got around people, I broke out in a rash from the stress. I got to the point that I was so wound up, I could not stop, sit down, or take a break.

"I realized something was wrong, so I went to see my doctor. He was a fine Christian man who told me that I needed to take medication for several months in order to get well. He did not want me to stop the treatment at any time. When I told him I didn't think it was spiritual to take medicine for this kind of problem, he said, 'If you broke your back, would you let me treat it to make you well? You wouldn't question whether it was spiritual to take medication for your back. This drug is a treatment to heal your body and mind.'"

Like many Christians who struggle with depression, Janet needed to hear that depression not only impacts us physically and emotionally, it also impacts us spiritually. I told her, "When I was depressed and having panic attacks, I could not pray. When I read the Bible I felt guilty, because I felt like a failure and could not do what it said. This is not unusual for a depressed person."

Janet nodded vigorously, identifying with me. I reminded her that she was God's beloved child, that her emotional and physical exhaustion had not caught Him by surprise. He understood what she was facing and wanted her to know His love in the middle of her struggle. Janet needed to know that, regardless of what she was feeling, God had not changed toward her—she was precious in His sight.

MEET HER FELT NEED

The next step for Janet was to take her list and pray through it out loud with me. I told her that she needed to tell God how she felt about every situation and pressure, and release each one into His hands.

We spent a long time in prayer as Janet expressed her anguish over the many difficult things in her life. There were long moments of silence as she struggled to let go of some of the pain, deep hurt, and drive to please everyone. She prayed, "Lord, I cannot manage our daughter. She wears me down emotionally and physically. I feel hopeless, weak, and helpless. I am panicked when I think of what she will become. I know You gave her to us, that she came from Your hand. Forgive me for giving up on her. Please take my hopelessness and give me hope. I put her and all the pain of dealing with her into Your care. I give it up to You."

At the end of our prayer time, she wiped the tears from her eyes and said, "It feels so good to have let go of everything and put it in God's hands, but will I be able to keep things from crowding in on me when I get back home and life is normal?"

Janet needed to make a plan for change. I took her to 1 Kings 18–19 to show her how God had dealt with someone in her same frame of mind. Elijah, God's prophet, also experienced depression. He was discouraged and full of self-pity. He was so down that he didn't even want to live. God did four things to treat Elijah's depression.

1. He put Elijah to sleep. Janet too had overextended and needed to pull in for a while. That required some changes in her schedule and mindset. I told her that they did not have to be permanent, only for a season, until she could regain her strength and perspective. I said, "Let's talk about what activities and responsibilities you can cut out." Because Janet was overwhelmed, she needed someone to take an unbiased look at her life and help her analyze what things she needed to change.

Janet didn't think she could eliminate anything from her schedule, because she was afraid someone would be hurt or disappointed. I asked her to make a list of all that she felt was expected of her. For each of her responsibilities, I asked her, "What are you the most afraid of? What is the very worst that could happen if you stop doing this for a while?" I wanted Janet to carefully look at what she feared and say it out loud.

As we talked, I explained that she did not always have to answer the phone and could choose a time each day to let the answering machine pick up. She could also stop entertaining for a while. I advised her not to say yes to giving dinner parties or any requests without first saying, "Give me a day to think and pray about it and I'll get back to you." Then she was to ask God what her motives would be if she accepted and if He would be pleased with her taking on another responsibility. I helped her plan some simple meals to cook for those times when she felt she really must have dinner guests.

2. He fed Elijah. A critical step on the road to recovery from depression and burnout is physical care. Janet needed to eat at least three balanced meals each day, starting with a good breakfast. I also suggested that she make a daily exercise plan, beginning with ten minutes a day and working up to thirty minutes if possible.

3. He encouraged Elijah. I said to Janet, "I want you to plan to do something fun for yourself every week. It may be something as little as taking a bubble bath while the kids are napping or something that requires more planning, like going out to eat with some girlfriends who will encourage you. Do something you enjoy. Go on a date with your husband, or spend some time in a bookstore, thrift shop, or on a hike."

4. He gave Elijah a helper to minister to him. Janet needed to find someone mature in the Lord who could pray with her and walk her through the depression. With help, Janet could take spiritual baby steps back to a strong relationship with God.

A depressed person needs spiritual encouragement. I told Janet that during my dark days I could not bring myself to read more than a verse or two in the Bible, and prayer took great effort. I suggested that she try a simple plan that helped me in my depression (see "Praying the Psalms" on page 123).

PRAYING THE PSALMS

- Start reading Psalms with chapter 1, verse 1.
- Read slowly, verse by verse, chapter by chapter. Visualize the words coming from God and through your spirit. Say each verse back to God as a prayer.
- Let the psalms put words in your mouth and heart that you may not have. They can express emotions that you may feel but are unable to identify.
- If what you are praying back to God is not true in your life, confess it. Praying the psalms can bring conviction.
- You will read statements about God, who He is, and who you are in Him. Let those be affirmations of what you believe about Him. If you feel you don't believe what you say, tell God that you want to believe.
- The psalmists often talk about enemies, even physical ones. As you pray the psalms, think of the enemies as those things you battle with in your soul. Psalm 83:17 says, "Let them be ashamed and dismayed forever; and let them be humiliated and perish." Your prayer of this verse can be, "Let the enemies of my soul—pride, selfishness, and so on—be dismayed forever. Let them die." You can use verses like this to come against your emotional and spiritual enemies, asking God to wipe them from your life.

After showing Janet what God did to minister to Elijah in his dark time, I told her, "If the depression continues after you have put the plan in place and have been on the medication a few weeks, you will need to see a professional counselor. Your pastor can recommend someone who is a believer you can trust to speak truth into your life. However, I believe that with the steps you have taken, God has already begun a healing work."

HELP HER BECOME INDEPENDENTLY DEPENDENT

Because of her emotional state, Janet's faith was weak. She questioned herself and God. She needed me to represent God's love and faithfulness to her until she could believe it for herself. But I wanted to give her something she could stand on, with or without anyone else's help. I said, "Janet, we've talked about things that will help you, but it won't be easy for you to make changes and take care of yourself. Still I know that God can help you return home and, in time, get back to your normal routines.

I want you to read 2 Corinthians 9:8 to me."

As Janet read the verse slowly, it was as if she was seeing it in a new light, "And God is able to make *all* grace *abound* to you, so that *always* having *all* sufficiency in *everything,* you may have an *abundance* for *every* good deed" (emphasis mine). The lavish promise of God's grace was something Janet could cling to when she faced the moments when she would be tempted to fall back into her depressed habits of thought.

I repeated the verse, stressing the words, emphasizing the promise. Then I painted a mental picture for her: "Think of God's grace as if it were in a bottle. Every time something happens and you think *I can't take this,* I want you to take that bottle of God's grace and pour it out on that situation saying, 'I have enough grace for this.' But when you stand the bottle back up, picture it *full.* God has promised that His grace would be abundant, more than enough. It will take time to break the cycle of responding the way you have, but if you face it with the truth of the 'All All' verse, you will put into practice a godly perspective on your circumstances."

Then I prayed, "Dear Lord, You see that Janet needs Your touch on her life. I pray that she will experience new peace as she returns home. Help her to see that she doesn't have to please everyone and do everything, but that she needs just to please You and to recognize that You will give her the strength for each day as You promised in Your Word. Help her to keep her priorities straight. And Lord, thank You that Your grace is sufficient for everything that she will have to face. I pray for renewal and refreshment as she returns home. In Jesus' name, amen."

Janet called a few days after she had returned home and said that her first day back had been great. The change of scenery and her new mindset had helped her manage the daily challenges that overwhelmed her in the past. However, she said, she fell flat on her face the second day. She told me that she retreated to her bathroom, shut the door, and cried out to God. "The image of the grace bottle came back to me—I have enough grace for everything, if I will just access it. I wondered how I could remember that in the pressured moments. I went to my kitchen, got a bottle, and filled it with water and food coloring. I put it in a place where I could look at it often and remind myself that God's grace is there for me always."

It has been more than ten years since Janet's visit. She struggled putting the Elijah plan in place at first. However, with God's help, a plan, medication, and the support of friends, she slowly pulled out of her depression. She called me recently to joyfully tell me that her daughter is doing well. Then she said, "I was in such a dark place when I visited you. But it was during that bleak time that I learned about God in a deep way. Sometimes praying the Psalms was like praying to the ceiling, but the discipline of it held me close to Him. I am so amazed because now God is bringing women to me who are in the same place I was all those years ago. I am thrilled that He is using the worst time in my life to encourage others. I would never want to go back to that time, but I would not trade it. I learned so much about myself and God. God is good."

difficult family members

WHAT YOU NEED TO KNOW

It's important to have boundaries with people whose actions are hateful or mean toward us. In order to gain self-respect and the respect of those who would take advantage of us, we need to set boundaries for relationships.

According to Drs. Henry Cloud and John Townsend, "A boundary is a personal property line that marks those things for which we are responsible."[1] In other words, each person needs to have well-defined limits in order to maintain personal integrity. For example, a woman can set a boundary that her parents can no longer make demeaning comments to her when she is talking with them.

The ability or inability to set boundaries has a great deal to do with the family environment one grows up in. Because of that, setting limits in relationships between family members can be particularly challenging. Cloud and Townsend write, "At first glance, it seems as if the individual who has difficulty setting limits is the one who has the boundary problem; however, people who don't respect others' limits also have boundary problems."[2] Family dynamics can blur those lines and make it difficult for a person to know how to protect herself from encroachment.

For insight into knowing how to help your counselees establish healthy boundaries, I recommend the book *Boundaries: When to Say Yes, When to Say No, to Take Control of Your Life* by Cloud and Townsend. It talks about what boundaries look like, how to develop them, how to deal with conflicts, and how to measure success. Other helpful resources by Drs. Cloud and Townsend are *Boundaries in Marriage* and *Boundaries Face to Face: How to Have That Difficult Conversation You've Been Avoiding.*

HELP AND HOPE FROM GOD'S WORD

Spend time reading and meditating on the following passages of Scripture, asking God to show you how you can use them to help someone who struggles with this issue.

Psalm 141:5

Proverbs 4:23; 9:8

Matthew 5:23-24

John 2:24-25

Ephesians 4:15,25,29-30

James 1:20

LANCE THE BOIL

When I asked Anne to tell me why she had come to see me, she began by telling me that she and her husband, Robert, had been married for five years. Before they were married, Anne's sister-in-law had been distant toward her but never rude. Anne had been sure that after she and Robert became husband and wife she would be able to win her sister-in-law's affection. But after five years she was a long way from her goal.

In fact, Robert's sister, Debbie, had made it clear that she did not like Anne. Whenever they were together at a family gathering, Debbie seemed to be at her cruelest, making fun of Anne and pointing out her faults. Robert and Debbie were the only two children and had been close when they were growing up.

Anne longed for her sister-in-law's approval because she felt that the lack of it was also affecting her relationship with Robert. Every time she came away from a visit with her husband's family she felt crushed. She thought, *Somehow I've got to change so I can win Debbie's acceptance.* Anne was beginning to despise Debbie, because she could not accomplish that goal.

MEET HER FELT NEED AND TAKE HER TO JESUS

After listening to Anne's story, I asked her if she had ever spoken to Debbie directly about the hurtful things she had said to her. "No," Anne replied, "I don't know if I could do it and keep from losing my temper or crying." Her silence with Debbie indicated that she had allowed the situation to develop that way because of inadequate boundaries. Anne needed help to know how to set limits to protect herself from repeated wounding.

"Anne, by not confronting Debbie you are acting as though everything is fine when it isn't. There are times when confrontation is necessary, especially if there is an ongoing problem. Healthy limits must be set when a person is being taken advantage of, disrespected, and so on. I'd like to give you some guidelines for godly confrontation."

Here is a summary of what I shared with her about how to confront someone.

Confrontation should never be done in anger. The Bible says, "The anger of man does not achieve the righteousness of God" (James 1:20). The way to be free of the anger is to work through forgiving those we are angry with. When we acknowledge to ourselves and to God the pain of someone's behavior toward us, we can begin to work on forgiving that person. This step toward confrontation is not to be brushed over lightly. Remember that forgiving means that we lift consequences and punishment from the offender. Forgiveness prepares the ground for today's battles and allows us to approach each interaction with a difficult person as a fresh start.

Confrontation doesn't bring healing or necessarily make us feel better. God is the one who heals us, and when we forgive and speak the truth in love, we've taken huge strides toward healing.

Confrontation should be done when we know the other party has something against us. This can bring healing to the relationship and ensures that our heart is right with God. Matthew reminds us, "Therefore if you are presenting your offering at the altar, and there remember that your brother has something against you, leave your offering there before the altar and go; first be reconciled to your brother, and then come and present your offering" (5:23-24). The goal in confronting someone is not to devastate or hurt, but to edify and help that person. To edify means to build and improve. Ephesians 4:29-30 tells us how to do that: "Let no unwholesome word proceed from your mouth, but only such a word as is good for edification according to the need of the moment, so that it will give grace to those who hear. Do not grieve the Holy Spirit of God."

When confronting use "I" statements rather than "you" statements. A "you" statement comes across as accusatory, so don't say, "*You* are causing problems. *You* are not treating me right." This puts a person on the defensive. Better to put the focus on yourself—what you need, feel, or want. For example, say something like this: "The tension between us at the Easter dinner has caused some problems for me. I am feeling misunderstood and hurt by what you said."

I warned Anne that confrontation does not guarantee that the situation will improve. In fact, it may even worsen. When a person has been obedient to God in speaking the truth in love and yet the other person makes no changes, further emotional boundaries must be established.

I said to Anne, "I want you to think about shifting your emotions into neutral when you are around Debbie. You can do this by choosing to refuse to take responsibility for her attitude and releasing to God all your expectations about her reaction to you. In other words, tell yourself, *So she's mad* or *She's unhappy with me. I will choose not to let it make a difference in my attitude.* You can pray, 'Lord, I will choose not to get upset and irritated or disappointed with Debbie. Help me to put into practice what You have been teaching me.' When you do this, you step away from the emotion and come to a place of detachment.

Christ set an example for dealing with difficult people: "Jesus would not entrust himself to them, . . . for he knew what was in a man" (John 2:24-25, NIV). I reminded Anne that all she had to do was to honor and respect Debbie as her husband's sister. She did not have to change, perform for her, or even like her. I encouraged her not to have any expectations of Debbie and not to spend much time in her company. I suggested that she regard her sister-in-law as she would a fine piece of furniture. A person would not scratch or abuse or knock it over, but it does not have to be a main focus.

I asked Anne to do a project on interpersonal relationships (see "Interpersonal Relationship Principles" to the right), because I wanted her to learn more about what Scripture has to say regarding relationships. When we keep God's principles in the forefront of the mind, it enables us to cultivate godly interaction with even the most difficult people.

"Anne, you can grow from Debbie's criticism of you," I told her, "if you handle it in a godly

INTERPERSONAL RELATIONSHIP PRINCIPLES

Read Ephesians 4 and Colossians 3 all the way through twice. On the second time around, note every relationship principle touched on in those chapters. For example, the principle set out in Colossians 3:14 is that we are to put on love ("the perfect bond of unity"). Then answer the following questions:

1. What point touched on an area of need in my life?
2. What difference would it make in my life if I followed the principles in Ephesians 4 and Colossians 3?
3. Which of these principles do I feel I live by well?

manner. Ask God to show you if there is any truth in what she says to you. Ask Him to help you to act on what is true and give the rest to Him."

The psalmist said in Psalm 141:5, "Let a righteous man strike me—it is a kindness; let him rebuke me—it is oil on my head. My head will not refuse it" (NIV). Painful relationships can be springboards for learning. The danger is that the hurt person will take what has been said to her and own it, regardless of whether it is true or not. That is a victory for Satan. Softness to a true rebuke is a sign of wisdom (see Proverbs 9:8). A mature Christian can ask God to help her discern if there is truth in the hurtful things that were said.

BELIEVE FOR HER

Anne and I met only a few times. Believing for her meant assuring her that there are godly ways to confront, that she could speak her mind in a way that was not sinful. It also included holding her accountable to speak even though it was difficult for her. I promised her that God would be with her when she confronted Debbie, even if she did not feel His presence. I committed to pray for her, particularly on the day of her next encounter with her sister-in-law.

Then I prayed with her, "Dear Lord, we know that You have brought Anne and her husband together. And You know the painful situation she is in. Thank You that You are aware of all of our hurts. I want to pray for special grace for Anne and strength as she confronts Debbie. Give her Your love for Debbie. I ask that she will be able to approach her and speak to her in a way that will bring about reconciliation. I pray that she will trust You while You are at work in Debbie's heart. Give her the grace to wait. Help her to be kind and able to walk through her circumstances in a Christ-like manner. We pray for Debbie that You will do a work in her heart, that You will help her to see why she is mistreating her sister-in-law, and that You will bring these two together in a way that would bless everyone. In Jesus' name, amen."

The last time I saw Anne I asked her how it was going. She laughingly told me, "My sister-in-law still doesn't like me, but I'm doing much better. It is still hard to go to family gatherings, but I feel like I am being true to myself and to the Lord."

fear

WHAT YOU NEED TO KNOW

Fear is a natural response to danger—either real or perceived—and can be characterized by dread, apprehension, or uncertainty. Without this God-given emotion, we would fail to protect ourselves in potentially life-threatening situations. Fear that springs out of a respect for danger is not wrong. It is God's tool of protection.

An exaggerated fear is a phobia. The dictionary calls it "a persistent, irrational fear of a specific object, activity, or situation that leads to a compelling desire to avoid it."[1] Paul refers to a phobia as the "spirit of fear" (2 Timothy 1:7, KJV). We exhibit a spirit of fear when the thing we are afraid of *controls* us. When we are controlled by something and become fearful, we lose our ability to trust God and sometimes we even doubt His love. This can affect our ability to think clearly.

Many people go underground with their fear because they do not know how to deal with it; they feel it is wrong or they are ashamed and try to hide it. As KTCs we need to discern whether a counselee is grappling with God-given fear and apprehension or is being battered by a spirit of fear.

New or difficult situations often create normal fear in a person. God does not expect us to encounter the difficult or unknown without fear. But even when we are terrified to face a new situation or assume a difficult responsibility, fear does not have to paralyze us. We must keep going forward with God, in trust.

HELP AND HOPE FROM GOD'S WORD

Spend time reading and meditating on the following passages of Scripture, asking God to show you how you can use them to help someone who struggles with this issue.

Psalm 23:4

Proverbs 29:25

Isaiah 41:10; 51:12

Romans 8:35

Ephesians 1:19-20

Philippians 4:13

2 Timothy 1:7

2 Peter 2:19

1 John 4:18-19

LANCE THE BOIL

When Candi, a darling, vivacious teenager, came to see me, she said, "My father calls me a worry wart. I live with the constant fear that bad things are going to happen to me and those I love. It's a dread that never goes away. Nothing seems to help. I find myself resisting anything that is new or different and that requires me to go someplace or do something I have not done before."

I asked Candi what she thought the root issues could be that were contributing to her fear. We talked about her childhood and anything that might play a role in making her feel so afraid. I inquired and probed about any hurtful situations that she had gone through that might not have been healed.

As Candi and I talked about her growing-up years, it became clear that she had an inordinate terror of being trapped by fire. Slowly, through answers to my questions, she revealed how the seed of fear had taken root in her heart. "When I was a little girl, I was playing outside a friend's house. She lived next door to a huge office building. I heard a lot of noise and shouting. When I looked up, I saw flames shooting out of the top two floors. While my friend and I watched, the people who were trapped up there began to get desperate and several of them jumped. We could hear the sirens getting closer and then the sirens began to fade. The fire trucks were trying to locate the building, while people jumped to their deaths. I felt so desperate and helpless. I don't know if anybody on the upper floors made it out alive."

What began as a healthy fear of fire had taken root and grown to the point that Candi had become anxious about many things, and fear was affecting her quality of life.

TAKE HER TO JESUS

When Candi finished, I said, "What a horrible thing to have gone through!" I wanted Candi to know that a scene like the one she had witnessed is truly awful and difficult to deal with. It was important that I not negate what came out of that experience when we talked about what she was fearful of now. I said to her, "I believe that your terrifying experience with the fire is the root of the fear that you are feeling now. You have taken on a spirit of fear because of the traumatic event you went through. Second Timothy 1:7 talks about that spirit: 'For God hath not given us the spirit of fear; but of power, and of love, and of a sound mind'" (KJV).

Fear is a natural, dominant emotion in most people, and I believe that is why God has so much to say about it in Scripture. Isaiah wrote,

> Do not fear, for I am with you;
> Do not anxiously look about you, for I am your God.
> I will strengthen you, surely I will help you,
> Surely I will uphold you with My righteous right hand."
> (41:10)

I wanted Candi to know that in these verses God was saying to her, "Candi, don't be controlled by fear. Take My hand and go forward."

I went on to tell her, "You can do that because He is with you. When He says to not 'anxiously look about,' it is because it is human and normal to look all around at the fearful situations that surround us. Do you believe that God was there with you the day of the fire?"

Candi answered hesitantly, "Yes, but what about the people who were trapped? I keep thinking that if they knew God, why didn't He save them? I worry that someday it could be me or someone I love in an impossible situation like that and maybe God won't come through."

I reminded Candi that the fire did not catch God by surprise. He even knew that the fire trucks were going to be delayed in getting there. I told her that I did not know why He let her go through the horror of watching people jump. "What we *do* know is that God was in control then, just as He is now."

I pointed to my Bible. "It says right here in Isaiah 41 that He *will* help you. That promise is regardless of the circumstances, and it is definite, because there are no maybes in the Bible. God does not expect you to follow any checklist. He simply says, 'I am your God, I will help you, I will uphold you with My hand.' When you feel yourself getting fearful, I want you to mentally picture Him holding your hand. That is His promise. There is no situation that He cannot handle."

Second Timothy 1:7 tells us what God wants to give *in place* of a spirit of fear. God says He gives "power, . . . love, and . . . a sound mind" (KJV). He can give us these things because He lives in us.

I passed my Bible over for Candi to read the following verses to me:

There is no fear in love; but perfect love casts out fear, because fear involves punishment, and the one who fears is not perfected in love. We love, because He first loved us. (1 John 4:18-19)

And what is the surpassing greatness of His power toward us who believe. These are in accordance with the working of the strength of His might which He brought about in Christ, when He raised Him from the dead and seated Him at His right hand in the heavenly places. (Ephesians 1:19-20)

When she finished reading I had Candi tell me what kind of power these verses say is available to her. I wanted her to grasp the true meaning of the passage so it would come back to her mind when she felt afraid. It is easy to just read a verse and not personalize it. Candi needed to know that God could give her His extraordinary power — power strong enough to raise Jesus from the dead — to come against the fear that gripped her.

BELIEVE FOR HER

When she was operating in fear, Candi could not sense God's presence with her. Each week when she came to see me, we talked about the times that she had felt afraid that week. One day she told me that her best friend wanted her to go to a weekend camp, but she was afraid to go. When I asked her why, she said, "I've never been there before. I won't know anybody except my friend. And we'll be way out in the middle of nowhere, and if something bad happens . . ."

I asked her gently where God was planning to be that weekend. When she answered that, of course, He would be with her, I looked steadily at her and said, "Do you believe that God can take care of what you are afraid might happen at the camp?" She said yes, but that she still felt afraid. My job then was to show her, believe for her, and underline that God is a trustworthy God. I told her this emphatically, because I knew it to be true. He would not abandon her. I assured her that when she didn't feel His presence, He was there. I thanked Him for His presence with her and pointed out evidence that He was caring for her from her own account of events in her life.

I met with Candi many times before she was able to consistently trust and rest in God's care for her. She needed me to be patient as she stepped out to trust God. Each time we met, we talked about her trust journey. When she had faced her fears well and met the challenge, we rejoiced together. When she struggled, I reminded her of what she had in her spiritual arsenal to combat the fears that sometimes threatened to control her.

HELP HER BECOME INDEPENDENTLY DEPENDENT

Candi experienced freedom from fear when she realized that she needed to trust and rest in God's sovereignty and care over her life. As she exercised her trust muscles, her ability to rest in God grew.

Candi decided to attend the weekend camp and to try to trust God with her fears. Afterward she told me that the trip there and the first night were hard, but she kept reminding herself of the truth that God held her hand. In the end, she said the weekend was a good experience.

As time passed she chose to face other unknown situations that initially caused her to feel panic. I prayed Candi through everything from visits to new doctors, to a road trip, to going away to college. I watched her develop an awareness of God's active, continual presence with her, even when bad things did happen.

Candi was a very sensitive person, and this worked against her when she faced the fears of living in a hard world. But God had created her with a caring spirit. As she learned to trust Him more and more, He began to use her to help other people find freedom from a spirit of fear.

grief

WHAT YOU NEED TO KNOW

Loss is a normal part of life, and it needs to be grieved. Any loss can cause grief, not just death.

As a KTC you may meet with women who express grief over a situation that you would not grieve personally. For instance, most of us would grieve deeply over the death of a loved one, but not everyone grieves over the loss of a pet, a home, their youth, a move, a valuable piece of jewelry, or a child leaving home.

When you are counseling with a woman who is grieving, keep in mind that the intensity of a person's grief is directly related to how that individual perceives the loss. Even though the loss may seem trivial to you, it may be truly overwhelming to your counselee. Be careful not to dismiss her feelings or denigrate them. Instead, offer her comfort and strength; show compassion and understanding.

Unresolved grief can lead to physical, mental, and psychological problems. You can help those in grief work through their loss by encouraging them to acknowledge what they have lost and to talk about their feelings. Many people do not want to hear about others' pain because they can't change it or make it better. But such a reaction can make the one in grief feel shut off. You will be a source of sweet comfort, even if the main thing you do is listen and "weep with those who weep" (Romans 12:15).

Keep in mind that one session will not be enough to help a woman work through her grief. Ask questions that will facilitate relief. For example, "Tell me how your mother died." "What is your fondest memory of her?" "What did you like the most about her?" "Describe your relationship." "Are there things you regret?" Expect your counselee to return over and over again to the same things. That is the way grief works—it's cyclical. You may feel impatient, but understand that repeated expression brings release to the grieving person.

For many years psychologists and other professionals have held to the idea that there are five stages of grief: denial, anger, bargaining, depression, and acceptance. Grieving people usually go through each of these stages, and many more, to be healed, but not necessarily in that order. People don't work through one stage, never to return to that stage again. It's possible to feel anger, move on to bargaining, and then return to the anger stage. Grieving is work.

An excellent resource book for dealing with any loss is *Let Me Grieve But Not Forever: A Journey Out of the Darkness of Loss* by Verdell Davis.

HELP AND HOPE FROM GOD'S WORD

Spend time reading and meditating on the following passages of Scripture, asking God to show you how you can use them to help someone who struggles with this issue.

Deuteronomy 30:19-20; 33:27
Psalms 34:17-19; 56; 66:9-12
Isaiah 40:11; 42:3; 43:2; 54:5-8

2 Corinthians 1:3-5

1 Peter 5:9-10

LANCE THE BOIL

Sharon came to see me during her first year of college. "I am twenty-nine years old and I have recently become a widow after one year of marriage. Just a few months ago, my husband, Brian, and I met at the beach for a picnic supper after work. We had a wonderful time. It was especially nice because we had argued before he left for work that morning. After we ate, he got in his car and said he'd see me at our house. I told him that I would stop by my mother's to pick up something and then come home. When I got to my mom's, the telephone was ringing. It was the police telling us that Brian had been killed in a car accident. Even though he and I had a good time at the beach before he died, I feel so badly because I didn't apologize to him for my nasty tone of voice that morning. What I said to him keeps ringing in my ears.

"I don't know how I am going to live without him. I have come to Multnomah Bible College to start my life over. But I need someone to walk me through my grief and help me understand how to face life and school on my own. Can you be here for me?"

Sharon had just moved to Portland, a place where no one knew her or what had happened to her. She needed to have someone she could talk to about the biggest wound in her life, and she had chosen to do that with me. After I assured her that I would love to be available to her, I spent the rest of that first session asking her questions about how she and Brian met, what attracted her to him, how long they had dated, and what qualities she loved most about him. I wanted her to tell me what she felt about Brian and the pain of losing him.

People in grief tell me that others usually tend to avoid the subject of their loss. They don't know what to say and they fear that talking about the departed loved one will cause more pain. It makes the grieving one feel like their loved one is forgotten, because people act as if he or she never lived. But that person is still a huge part of her heart and life. She must have a place to express her thoughts in order to bring relief and healing.

MEET HER FELT NEED

The next time Sharon came to see me, I said, "Last time you mentioned that you have some regrets because you left things unsaid. Let's work on that today. Tell me about the argument you had the morning Brian died." If a person's grief is complicated by regret, her suffering will be intensified. Sharon needed to acknowledge the pain of her regrets—harsh words not made right, kind deeds left undone, unkind actions, and so on.

Sharon described what would have been an insignificant disagreement on any normal day. She was crying when she told me, "I just wish I could tell him I'm sorry and that I did want to keep my car cleaner, especially if that made him happy. But I was too worn out to think about cleaning my car, so I got mad at him for not understanding and never told him how I really felt."

"Why don't we work on telling him right now?"

Though it might take longer than the hour we had scheduled, I asked her to make a list of all the regrets she had about her relationship with Brian, beginning with her regret for not telling him she was sorry for their disagreement. Then, after she had listed the regrets, I asked her to make a list of all the things that she loved and appreciated about Brian. We both cried as she talked about the many things she loved about her young husband.

When that second list was finished, we knelt together with the two lists in front of us. Sharon sobbed as she poured out her regrets to God and asked Him to tell them to Brian. She cried even harder as she expressed to God all the things she loved and treasured about the young man she had lost. "Please tell him thank you from me and that I love him."

When her crying subsided, I said, "Sharon, now that you've told God everything, I want you to trust Him to take care of those regrets. Second Timothy 1:12 says, 'For I know the one in whom I trust, and I am sure that he is able to guard what I have entrusted to him until the day of his return'" (NLT).

When she asked me how to do that, I told her that each time any painful regret came to mind, she should stop it at the first reminder and simply say to the Lord, "I have given to You my failures and I will not take them back on myself. I want to thank You now for the privilege You have given me to have Brian in my life even for a short time." If she could constantly turn those painful thoughts to praise, it would be like balm to her hurting heart.

TAKE HER TO JESUS

One day Sharon came to see me unexpectedly. When I opened the door and saw her expression, I knew that she was in agony. I silently prayed, "Lord, I don't know what to say to her. She seems to be in so much anguish, I don't know if anything could comfort her except the arms of her husband." As Sharon paced the floor she sobbed, "I can't go on without Brian!"

I felt God guiding me to have her sit down and lean back on the big, soft chair I have in my office. As Sharon sat down, I asked her to close her eyes. "I want you to know what the Bible says in Deuteronomy 33:27: 'The eternal God is a dwelling place, and underneath are the everlasting arms.' Wherever the chair is touching your body I want you to visualize that it is the Lord Jesus holding you. What do you need right now from Him? Do you need to be comforted? Ask God to pour His comfort into you."

I waited for a minute or two and then asked, "Do you need love? Ask God to pour His love into you."

A few minutes later I said, "Do you need peace? Ask Him to give you peace now."

Sharon's shoulders heaved as she prayed silently, but slowly she grew calm as she began to feel God's arms around her. After a few minutes, she opened her eyes and said, "I am going to be okay now."

"When is the hardest time of day for you to be without Brian?" I asked.

"At night. During the day I keep very busy. But at night when I go to bed, I feel desperately lonely."

"When you go to sleep tonight I want you to remember Isaiah 40:11: 'He tends his flock like a shepherd: He gathers the lambs in his arms and carries them close to his heart' (NIV). When you put your head on your pillow, I want you to visualize that you are putting your head on God's chest, next to His heart."

I talked with Sharon about the fact that it takes three to five years for one who has lost a spouse to be able to see the sun shine again. "Sharon, I know that you expect to miss Brian on special days. But you need to be prepared that there will be times when you will be overwhelmed with grief when you don't expect it. Anything can trigger your grief: a whiff of his aftershave, a picture of a place the two of you enjoyed together, or someone who reminds you of him. When feelings of grief wash over you, don't stuff them down or push them away. Instead go to the Lord with your anguish and tell Him what you are feeling. When you are especially lonely and it seems like others have gone on with their lives, He is always there for you."

I turned to Isaiah 43:2 and asked her to read it to me:

> When you pass through the waters, I will be with you;
> And through the rivers, they will not overflow you.
> When you walk through the fire, you will not be scorched,
> Nor will the flame burn you.

When she finished I said, "Hold onto the Lord in the waters and fire of your pain. Picture Him next to you in the empty seat or walking along beside you and enjoying or suffering things with you. Acknowledge His presence, especially when life is hard."

BELIEVE FOR HER

Sharon and I met together for many months, and then I began to feel that she had become stuck in her grief. At times it appeared that she didn't want to be healed. Her identity had been in being Brian's wife, and she seemed to want to stay in that emotional frame of mind. As her mentor I had the responsibility to warn her of the danger of despair.

I said very tenderly, "Sharon, grief can dominate a person's life and rule the emotions to the point of keeping her from being able to function or heal. I don't want that to happen with you."

I have seen people who have allowed their loss to become like an idol, more important than their relationship with God. God's call to all of us who believe is "You shall have no other gods before Me" (Deuteronomy 5:7). Everything that touches the life of the believer comes through God's divine protection. All that touches the Christian is Father-filtered.

Moses told the Israelites,

I call heaven and earth to witness against you today, that I have set before you life and death, the blessing and the curse. So choose life in order that you may live, you and your descendants, by loving the LORD your God, by obeying His voice, and by holding fast to Him; for this is your life and the length of your days, that you may live in the land which the LORD swore to your fathers, to Abraham, Isaac, and Jacob, to give them. (Deuteronomy 30:19-20)

When we give our heartaches as a love gift to God, we are choosing life. We are saying to God, "I love You more than I love my right to hang on to my loss, to be angry, to stomp around, to be debilitated, to feel sorry for myself, and to question You."

After months of living in a debilitated state, and after she understood Moses' call to the Israelites to choose life, Sharon began to realize that she had allowed Brian's death to dominate everything in her life. She came to the determination that choosing life meant that she needed to limit her time of grieving each day. She set aside thirty minutes every day to cry, wail, shout, and remember. Then she gave up to God her right to grieve the rest of the day, thereby choosing blessing. Her love gift to God was yielding her right to change her circumstances or have her life different. She made this choice because she loved God more than she loved herself. It wasn't that she felt it was wrong to miss Brian—it wasn't—but her decision helped her continue to work through her grief and yet move on with her life.

Sharon let go of Brian one small step at a time. This carried her forward so that she could begin to reach out for any piece of new life she could find. One day we both realized that Brian had taken his rightful place in her life. While he would always be a part of her past and while his part in her life had changed her for the better, she was finally able to accept that he would not be a part of her future.

married and tempted

WHAT YOU NEED TO KNOW

Women are seldom tempted to have an affair because they are physically attracted to someone, but emotional connections and deep conversations with the opposite sex easily seduce the female heart. Because of this, women who are not being wooed and romanced by their husbands can be tempted to have an affair. When a wife is struggling because of her husband's lack of attention, it is very serious. She needs to tell him.

When a woman comes to you about her marriage, you may think, *I can't do anything because her husband needs to be here.* This isn't the case. God can work in her life, with or without the cooperation of her husband. While her felt need is her dissatisfaction with her marriage, the real need is her walk with God. You can help her deal with the problems in her marriage if she lets God participate in her circumstances.

The following questions can help you identify some underlying issues that may need to be dealt with in your counseling sessions:

- Does she exhibit the normal pain brought on by disappointment or difficult circumstances, or does she have an ungodly, bitter spirit?
- Does she show disrespect for her husband?
- Can something be done about her marital difficulties? Does she need to talk with her husband about how she feels? If she already has, how did he respond? If she hasn't talked with him, what is her reason? Talk with her about how to confront (see pages 108–109 and 129–131).
- Has she kept short accounts (see Ephesians 4:25-26), or has she let things mount up? (Note that if she doesn't keep short accounts, this Scripture says the Devil has an opportunity to come between her and her husband.)
- Did something happen between them before they were married that she is ashamed, embarrassed, or not proud of? Seek to discern what the root problem is.

Some excellent resources on this issue are *Intimate Issues*, by Linda Dillow and Lorraine Pintus, and *Intimacy Ignited*, by Dr. Joseph and Linda Dillow and Dr. Peter and Lorraine Pintus.

HELP AND HOPE FROM GOD'S WORD

Spend time reading and meditating on the following passages of Scripture, asking God to show you how you can use them to help someone who struggles with this issue.

Ecclesiastes 11:1

Matthew 5:27-28; 7:12

1 Corinthians 7:3-5; 10:13

Ephesians 4:25-26

Colossians 3:14

2 Timothy 2:22

LANCE THE BOIL

When I asked Ruth why she had asked to meet with me, she said that her marriage was in trouble. After ten years of marriage, she had recently gone back to work because things were tight financially. She and her husband didn't want the extra income to go toward child care, so they agreed that Ruth would work nights so that one of them would be at home at all times to take care of their three kids.

When I asked her to tell me more about why their marriage was in trouble, she said, "Since I started back to nursing, little things about my husband bother me that never used to. I don't feel like we know each other anymore, and when I am with him I feel lonely. He is not mean or nasty, but he doesn't pay much attention to me—and when he does, it seems like it's only because he wants sex.

"I think I'm falling in love with a male nurse who works with me. He is not handsome or spectacular in any way. But in quiet moments and on breaks we talk a lot. I don't know what happened or how it happened, but I'm very attracted to him and am having all sorts of crazy ideas about going away with him somewhere. I am a Christian and I know that what I am thinking doesn't please God, but what do I do with these feelings?"

MEET HER FELT NEED

As I listened to her story, I realized that Ruth not only needed help regarding what to do about the man she was emotionally involved with at work, but she also needed to address the distance that had grown between her and her husband. First I had to know whether she wanted to stay in the marriage. This was an important piece of information because I could not work with her unless she was willing to give up the other man. Sometimes a counselee will come for help with an issue that she is not truly ready to do something about. I needed to know for sure that Ruth was willing to give up the enticement of the attention from the other man, so I asked her, "Am I right in thinking that you don't want to break up your marriage over this other man?"

Ruth hesitated, then she said, "A part of me knows that what I am feeling is a school-girl crush. I think if things were better in my marriage, it wouldn't have been so easy to get attached to the man at work. I want to do the right thing."

If Ruth had told me she wasn't sure that she wanted to give up the other man, then at that point I would have had to address her relationship to God and what would please Him. The question is, who does she want to please most, God or herself?

Ruth's heart had been seduced by the intimate communication she was having with the male nurse. Very few, if any, women who are happy in their marriage and who say that they have a deep level of communication with their husbands are tempted to have a close emotional and/or sexual relationship with another man. I wanted to educate Ruth about what had made her emotionally vulnerable to temptation and then help her deepen the communication she had with her husband.

I said to her, "There are many levels of communication, but I will boil it down to three in order to keep it simple." I went on to explain that level 1 of communication, which is the most superficial, is fact sharing or the exchange of necessary information. For example, a fact-sharing conversation might go something like this:

Wife: "What are you going to do this morning?"

Husband: "I need to change the oil in my truck and pick up my shirts at the cleaners. What's your morning look like?"

Wife: "I need to finish the laundry and take Billy to his Little League practice. If I have time I'd like to stop at the hospital and visit Ellie. She's recovering well from her surgery but will be in the hospital for another week or so."

While level 1 communication is necessary and normal, it doesn't build intimacy in marriage, because neither person has revealed his or her heart. This level of communication has no mental, spiritual, or emotional depth.

The second level of communication, which is more personal, is the sharing of ideas, concepts, and opinions.

Wife: "What did you think about what the pastor said this morning?"

Husband: "I felt like he had to stretch to make his point. The issue is less black and white than he made it out to be, because Scripture is just not clear on this issue."

Level 2 communication deepens the connection between two people because they are communicating some of *who they are* to each other. When someone tells you his or her ideas and thoughts, it causes you to draw closer to that person and gives you a sense that you know how that individual thinks and responds to certain things on an intellectual level.

Level 3, the sharing of hurts, needs, wants, feelings, dreams, and desires, is the most intimate type of communication. Most women long for this level of communication in their marriages.

Wife: "I am so worried about the kids. I am afraid that they are growing away from us. They seem to be choosing odd friends and excluding us more and more."

Husband: "I know. I wish there were something we could do as a family that they could enjoy without too much of a fuss."

Wife: "When they grow up, I want them to want to be with us. Do you think that will happen?"

In general, women find it easier to engage in this deeper level of intimacy than do men.

After I'd summarized the levels of communication, I said, "Ruth, you have entered into level 3 communication with this man at work. You have shared your heart with him in ways that I suspect you have not done for a long time with your husband. The first thing you need to do is get away from this male nurse at your work."

Ruth looked surprised. "That seems a little drastic. I think I can be around him without going any further with the relationship. Besides, I need this job!"

"The Bible says, 'Run from anything that stimulates youthful lust' (2 Timothy 2:22, NLT). If you don't run from this temptation, you will be in greater danger of falling than you realize. If you are serious about wanting to please God, you *must* remove yourself from temptation. Let's brainstorm about your options."

Like many counselees I meet with, Ruth needed help in seeing that she did have some options. So I discussed with her the possibilities of getting a job at another hospital, of changing to another shift, and even of not working at all.

Toward the end of our time together, I said, "There is much more we need to work on. But at this point the most important thing for you to do is to take the necessary steps to end your relationship with this man. If you have to work any more shifts with him, I want you to be polite and impersonal toward him. Do not tell him that you need to cut off communication with him — simply do it. If you try to explain, you will be engaging in level 2 or even level 3 communication, and you'll be dancing with temptation once again. You don't owe this man an explanation. But you do owe one to your husband. What do you think you should tell him?"

I knew it would be very painful for Ruth's husband to hear that she felt she was falling in love with another man, so I wanted to coach her in what to say so that she would not lose his trust over something that she had thought about, but not yet acted out. I encouraged her to say something like this: "I am having a problem that I need to talk to you about. I am feeling like you and I are not spending enough time communicating and having heart talks. I am missing you deeply. I work with men at the hospital who often tell me about their thoughts and feelings. I need to get away from one man in particular. I really don't want my heart to be drawn away from you. I think that could happen if I am feeling lonely. I am really missing our times together." I also told her that if she did act on the temptation in the future, she would have to confess that.

When Ruth came back to see me the next week, she told me that her husband had been surprised, confused, and somewhat hurt by what she had told him. But he had agreed that she should make a change in her job, and she had already talked to the supervisor about a shift change. There were no openings on other shifts, but the supervisor told her she could move to another floor right away, which she did. Ruth said, "I like the new floor and I just make sure that I take my break when I know he won't be there."

I applauded Ruth's efforts and suggested that we turn our attention to improving her relationship with her husband. I asked her to tell me about him. As she talked, I listened for the things that she complained about. She told me that they had differences about how to deal with their finances and their children. She also said that he was extremely picky about some things but not about some of the things that bothered her, such as throwing his clothes on the floor.

I asked Ruth if she had talked with her husband about those differences. She said, "I have tried, but I never get anywhere, and I am afraid of making him angry." I encouraged her to discuss with him the issues that were bothering her, because a simple thing can become a big deal if it is not addressed. "Even if he gets angry, your relationship is too important to let these things cause a rift. Let's talk about some ways you can approach him and some possible compromises you could suggest to him."

Then I asked Ruth to tell me how these tensions had affected their physical relationship. She replied, "Well, we certainly aren't as sexually active as we used to be. It seems like I am mad at him all the time and don't even want to be close. I know that a wife needs to meet her husband's physical needs, so we make love once a week or so, but I don't enjoy it."

To help her better understand the role of sexual intimacy in marriage, I said, "When you look at a door, you see the frame, the doorknob, the color of the wood, but very seldom do you notice the hinges. Although you may not see them, the hinges are critical for the working of the door. Just as hinges are essential for the function of a door, so is the sexual relationship in marriage. The one thing God has made uniquely for marriage is the uniting of a man and woman in sexual oneness. Anyone could be a confidant, a companion, housekeeper, and a child-care provider. But God gave you to each other for the sharing of physical and emotional intimacy."

I went on to explain that when a man and woman's personalities and spirits click, and when they have compatible goals and values and are sexually attracted to each other, they fall in love. In marriage, the sexual act brings all those things together in a spiritual reaffirmation. God intended for marital sex to be physically pleasurable, as well as to confirm and express heart connections. A wife needs to connect with her husband physically if she wants to meet his emotional needs. If the sexual relationship of a marriage is not good, the emotional relationship will dissipate.

TAKE HER TO JESUS

I gave Ruth my Bible and asked her to find 1 Corinthians 7:3-5 and read it to me.

> The husband must fulfill his duty to his wife, and likewise also the wife to her husband. The wife does not have authority over her own body, but the husband does; and likewise also the husband does not have authority over his own body, but the wife does. Stop depriving one another, except by agreement for a time, so that you may devote yourselves to prayer, and come together again so that Satan will not tempt you because of your lack of self-control.

I looked at Ruth and asked, "The Bible points out that a physical relationship with your husband should be a priority. Have you thought about the fact that you have been depriving your husband of what is his? Have you thought that he might struggle with temptation?"

Ruth looked shocked at the suggestion that her husband might be tempted to stray. "It never crossed my mind. I would be devastated if he wanted someone else."

I said, "This passage says clearly that Satan takes advantage when couples deny each other the intimacy of lovemaking. I have seen this confirmed over and over. A few years ago my husband and I were doing a marriage conference, and Norm was talking with the men about their sex lives. One man wept and said, 'I am being tempted daily by every skirt that walks by because my wife won't let me touch her. All I really want is my wife.'

"Ruth, your brain is your most important sex organ. The pleasure that you will be able to receive and give is impacted directly by how you think about sexual intimacy. You are tired from caring for kids and working, and I bet you don't have much strength left over. I want you to know that your energy for sex will come from mentally choosing to take pleasure in it rather than feeling sorry for yourself or feeling imposed upon. Lovemaking can actually energize you and make you feel better about yourself. Try giving him signals that you are inviting him to intimacy, such as touching and hugging and warm verbal expressions in person or on the phone."

Ruth needed to take her focus off the fact that she hadn't been feeling attracted to her husband and begin to concentrate on how she could be attractive to him, so we talked about ways she could do that. I suggested that she consider buying some lingerie that would show off her curves and make her feel sensual. I reminded her not to point out her physical flaws to her husband, because he might see them in a new light and agree with her. I also brainstormed with her about how she could prepare their bedroom so that she would feel romantic in it. I told her that a candle, some music, and a sweet fragrance can help a lot.

"Coming together sexually revitalizes a sense of masculinity to the man and femininity to the woman. Even if you do not experience a big response, you can have the pleasure of knowing that you have brought your husband satisfaction. Sex can restore romance, tenderness, and life to your marriage."

During another visit I asked Ruth about how she and her husband treated each other. She quickly replied, "He doesn't treat me nicely."

Once again I took her to Jesus by showing her what the Bible says about how we are to treat others. "Jesus said that we are to treat others the way we want them to treat us. Matthew 7:12 says, 'In everything, therefore, treat people the same way you want them to treat you.' The Golden Rule is one of the keys to life and relationships, not just marriage. If you need compliments, you give them; if you need surprises, you can surprise."

There is something very healing to the heart when a woman gives to others what she needs herself. Ecclesiastes 11:1 says, "Cast your bread on the surface of the waters, for you will find it after many days." When a woman gives 100 percent to her husband without expecting anything in return, it will come back to her in blessing.

Common courtesies can often go by the wayside in marriage. Couples can get too comfortable with each other and forget to say, "Please," "Thank you," "Excuse me," "I'm sorry," and so on. I often hear couples speaking to one another in a negative tone of voice that they would not dare use with a stranger. When I asked Ruth if she had fallen into that trap, she answered, "But my husband talks to me even worse than I talk to him."

I challenged her to stop the cycle and to discipline herself to treat her husband with the courtesy that she desires for herself. I encouraged her to affirm him verbally, and then asked her to tell me some nice things about him.

Ruth looked at me blankly, so I told her about a woman I had met with who had decided she couldn't live with her husband any longer. This woman was unable to appreciate any value in her husband whatsoever because the things she didn't like about him filled her focus. I asked her to make a list of all the things she disliked about him on one side of a paper and then write down all the things she liked and respected about him on the other side. She quickly filled the negative side but struggled to come up with anything positive. Finally, I asked her, "Does your husband shower?"

She was shocked. "Of course he does!"

"Then write that down. Some women live with men who do not bathe or brush their teeth. You are so focused on the bad things you see in your husband that you cannot recognize that you have much to be thankful for."

Ruth laughed at my story and then looked serious. "You're right. I get so busy thinking about the negative things that I forget why I married him. I get blinded to the man he really is."

Ruth went on to list some of those positive qualities. When she had finished, I challenged her to start saying some of them to her husband. "If a positive thought comes into your mind about him, try to remember to tell him."

Then I added, "The other thing I want you to do is to make the decision to love him. Look up Colossians 3:14 and read it to me." She read, "Beyond all these things put on love, which is the perfect bond of unity."

"Why would God want us to be loving if we don't feel love toward someone?" I asked. I went on to explain, "I think it is because He made us with both will and emotions. He knew that we cannot keep the two apart for very long. If we act with our emotions, our will follows, and if we act with our will, our emotions follow. You can 'put on love' by acting it out with your will, until you feel it."

Ruth began to try out some of the ideas we had talked about. When she returned for our next meeting, she said she was surprised at her husband's response to her and that he was more tender with her. She said, "I even feel that if I can keep this acting thing going, I might get my feelings back."

BELIEVE FOR HER

Because Ruth had tasted forbidden excitement, she was struggling with believing that her marriage could ever be exciting to her. I knew it could, if she made wise, godly choices. I had to represent that to her and teach her how she could revitalize her passion for her husband. My role as a KTC was to take Ruth to the Truth. I was there to listen to her and hold out hope and encouragement when she expressed doubt.

Believing for Ruth meant that I constantly reminded her of who God is. When a person struggles with trusting God to bring about change in her life, the KTC can point her to God, who walks with her. Ruth needed to be reminded and reassured that God wanted her to walk in purity before Him, that He would honor the godly choices that she made. "He wants you to have a good marriage," I said. "If you will be faithful, God will work. Remember, you are in a process. Your heart will catch up with the decisions you have made with your will."

HELP HER BECOME INDEPENDENTLY DEPENDENT

Because Ruth had told her husband that she was missing him emotionally and that she needed to get away from temptation, it served as a wake-up call for him. When she began to show interest in him again, it slowly rekindled their romance. When Ruth would slip back into critical thinking about her husband, I reminded her of the close call she'd had. I told her that keeping the Lord in the forefront of her mind and cultivating intimacy with the Lord Jesus would help her stay true. Recently she told me, "I am committed to this marriage."

married to an unbeliever

WHAT YOU NEED TO KNOW

If a woman is married to a man who isn't interested in growing spiritually or is an unbeliever, she may feel discouraged, defeated, and hopeless about the future. Some believe the marriage is out of God's will.

Encourage her to do the following:

- Live with her husband in an understanding way.
- Choose to honor and respect him.
- Trust the Holy Spirit to work in his life.
- Practice the marriage principles set out in Scripture.
- Not portray herself as a pitiful person because she lives with a nonbeliever.
- Remember that God promises to be her protection and her husband.

Stand with her in prayer for her husband's salvation, encourage her to be thankful, and let God meet her heart needs.

HELP AND HOPE FROM GOD'S WORD

Spend time reading and meditating on the following passages of Scripture, asking God to show you how you can use them to help someone who struggles with this issue.

1 Kings 10:16-17; 14:25-28

2 Chronicles 14:11

Psalm 37:1-5

Proverbs 14:1; 24:3-4

Isaiah 42:16; 54:5; 64:6

Matthew 19:4-9

Romans 12:3

1 Corinthians 2:9; 7:13

Ephesians 1:1-14; 3:20; 5:33

1 Peter 3:1

LANCE THE BOIL

I had known Amy during her college years, but when she graduated, we lost touch. A few years later she called and asked if she could come to see me. When she arrived, I could tell she was distressed and sad. "Amy, tell me what's on your heart," I said. Here is what she told me.

"After I left school I worked for two years as a store manager. I went to church and attended the singles group. The guys in the group were all kind of odd, and I just didn't click with anybody. One day at work, the district manager brought along his new assistant, Phil, for a meeting. I thought Phil was nice and really good-looking. When he called and asked me out to dinner, I thought it might be store business, but it wasn't long before I realized he was interested in me. He said he was a Christian, but I knew by what he told me that he wasn't living like one. But he was really nice and went to church with me, so I kept seeing him.

"We went out for a few months and fell in love. When Phil asked me to marry him, I didn't really pray about it. I think I was probably afraid God would tell me not to go ahead with it. I kept thinking, *This will work. I'll be good for him and he will grow in his walk with God.* I felt a little anxious and almost uncomfortable about marrying Phil, but I went ahead anyway, and we were married in my church two years ago.

"It wasn't long before I knew that Phil wasn't serious about his Christian life. He stopped going to church with me right after the wedding, and now I don't see any evidence that he even believes in God. I love him, but I have become very unhappy. I am so sad. I feel like I have disappointed God because I went against what He was telling me and married Phil anyway. Now I am mad at Phil for misleading me and for not walking with God. I am totally defeated. I let his charm and good looks sidetrack me from the Christian marriage that I had always dreamed of. I don't feel like I can do anything for God now. Am I going to always live a life out of His will? What do I do?"

Like many women in her situation, Amy was struggling with several things. One area of difficulty was how to treat her husband, because she felt he had misled her. I opened my Bible to Ephesians 5:33, which says, "The wife must see to it that she respects her husband," and pointed out that the verse says nothing about the husband's spiritual condition. The passage makes it clear that God's blueprint for wives is to honor their husbands because of their God-given position as head of the family, regardless of their spiritual state.

Amy acknowledged that she was struggling to honor Phil because he wasn't responding well to her attempts to bring Him to Christ. Christian women married to nonbelievers or immature Christians can fall into the deadly trap of showing disapproval of their husbands through looks and facial expressions that say, "I am disappointed in you." They make remarks about things their husbands do that they think are sinful, and they beg and plead with their husbands to go to church.

A psychological study of married couples by Dr. John Gottman, author of *The Mathematics of Divorce*, found that if one partner or the other conveyed contempt, it was highly likely that the marriage would end in divorce. He discovered that the four most deadly attitudes in a marriage are defensiveness, stonewalling, criticism, and contempt. If one or both partners in a marriage show contempt toward the other, it signals that the marriage is in trouble. According to Gottman, contempt is any statement made with a superior attitude.[1]

Christian women, whether they are married to a nonbeliever or not, often feel they need to bring conviction to their husbands. This almost never works. These wives communicate an attitude of superiority, and this is something wives are cautioned against in Scripture. When a woman sets herself up as a spiritual judge, she violates God's words in Romans 12:3 to not think of herself more highly than she ought. After all, Isaiah 64:6 says that human righteousness is as "filthy" rags in God's eyes.

Peter wrote, "If any of them do not believe the word, they may be won over *without words* by the behavior of their wives" (1 Peter 3:1, NIV, emphasis mine). I showed Amy this passage and then said, "You need to trust the Holy Spirit to work in Phil's life and convict him — that's not your job. It will be counterproductive for you to quote Scripture or scold him for doing ungodly things. Don't say anything to your husband; instead pray for his salvation. Ask God to love Phil through you. Choose to delight in him every way you can."

I went on to encourage Amy not to portray herself to others as a woman to be pitied because she is married to a nonbeliever. I pointed out that one way she could honor Phil was by not discussing him or his lack of faith with others, including people at church. I encouraged her to find one or two trusted prayer warriors who would pray for her husband and support her. Paul told Timothy, "The Lord will give you understanding in everything" (2 Timothy 2:7), and He would also show Amy what to say to the prayer warriors.

TAKE HER TO JESUS

Not only did Amy need help in learning how to treat Phil, she also needed to know that even if she had been out of God's will in her decision to marry him, God viewed her marriage to Phil as sacred. Matthew wrote, "So they are no longer two, but one flesh. What therefore God has joined together, let no man separate" (19:6).

I asked her to read me that verse and then said, "Your marriage to Phil is God's will for your life now. Put aside any more thoughts or conversation about being out of God's will, because that will defeat you. First Corinthians 7:13-14 says, 'And a woman who has an unbelieving husband, and he consents to live with her, she must not send her husband away. For the unbelieving husband is sanctified through his wife, . . . otherwise your children are unclean, but now they are holy.'"

Women who believe they have disobeyed God by marrying the wrong man feel guilty. When things become difficult in their marriage, they wonder if God is punishing them for their disobedience. They fear that if they stepped out of God's will by marrying, then they are forever bound to living out of God's will unless they dissolve that union. However, I don't believe this is what Scripture teaches. Once a couple walks through the marriage door (even if it was out of disobedience) the marriage becomes God's will for them.

I told Amy this and said, "Before the foundation of the world, God knew you would choose to marry Phil—and He still chose you to be His daughter. Please read Ephesians 1:4-12."

After Amy had read the Ephesians passage to me, we talked about how it applied to her situation. I wanted her to know that God's desire for her was to live for the praise of His glory; no matter the situation she was in right then, He wanted her to show His beauty in her marriage.

Proverbs 14:1 tells us, "The wise woman builds her house, but the foolish tears it down with her own hands." A woman who leaves an unbelieving man tears down her house. As painful as an unequal yoke may be, God will work in the middle of it. His goal is to conform us to His image. Satan, on the other hand, is going to do everything he can to make the woman who disobeyed God feel that she is far from Him because her marriage is not aligned with a godly standard. I said to Amy, "You are ashamed about going against God and angry and hurt over Phil. You cannot feel God's nearness when you carry emotions like that. You are just where Satan wants you. Don't let him push you away from God. Now is when you especially need Him."

Then I had her read Ephesians 3:20 to me, which says that God is "able to do far more abundantly beyond all that we ask or think, according to the power that works within us." I encouraged Amy to ask God to work in Phil and to trust that He would. She needed to be reminded that God can change anyone, even an unbelieving husband. She needed to accept the fact that even if Phil never changes, Jesus will be sufficient for her. I assured her that she could choose to live with Phil in a godly manner and honor the Lord. "God can help you make your marriage good, even if it may not be what you dreamed. He will help you make your family the most Christlike it can be."

I supported this promise with a story from 1 Kings 10:16-17 and 14:25-28. King Solomon, who was incredibly wealthy, had five hundred solid-gold shields made. The shields not only were beautiful but also offered protection from Israel's enemies. Years later, Shishak, the king of Egypt, came and stole all of Israel's treasures out of the palace and the temple, including the gold shields. When Rehoboam became Israel's king, he replaced the stolen shields with bronze ones. Bronze was not as valuable or as beautiful as gold, but it was attractive and could still be used for protection.

After I told her the story, I said, "Amy, I believe that God wants to make something beautiful out of your home. Your marriage may not be made of gold, but it can be like those bronze shields. It can still be good and a protection for you and the children you hope to have. Phil may be the wheel of the family, but you, as the wife, are the hub. Everything revolves around you. Because of your powerful influence, you can set an atmosphere of peace and happiness in your home. You can choose to be content with what you have. If you are firmly grounded and assured that you are beloved of God, He will meet your needs."

BELIEVE FOR HER

When she first came to see me, Amy had no hope that she could ever rest in God's plan for her because she had been responsible for messing it up. She constantly beat herself up for going against God's word to her when she married Phil. She struggled with trusting God that the disappointment of her broken dreams could ever be eased.

I often told her, "Amy, you have said several times that you don't have the marriage you always dreamed of. Psalm 37:1-5 gives principles that you can apply to your disappointment." This passage lays out the following pattern of a godly response to broken dreams:

- Do not fret (verse 1)
- Trust and keep doing what is right (verse 3, my paraphrase)
- Dwell in the land and cultivate faithfulness (verse 3)
- Delight yourself in the LORD; and *He will give you the desires of your heart* (verse 4, emphasis mine)
- Commit your way to the LORD, trust also in Him, and *He will do it* (verse 5, emphasis mine)

According to these verses, our focus must be on God rather than on the dreams that lie broken at our feet. We can choose to trust—not fret—and to do what is right in God's eyes. I told Amy, "When you do those things, you put yourself in a place to delight in God. You can commit yourself to Him and trust Him. Even if you are not living your dream marriage, you can build your house with wisdom, understanding, and knowledge, according to the guidelines set out in Proverbs 24:3-4. Those are things God promises you if you will ask and seek Him."

HELP HER BECOME INDEPENDENTLY DEPENDENT

I met with Amy for many months, and whenever she hit a rough spot, we would talk. She needed to be weaned from regular counseling because no one could live her marriage for her. She had to learn to live trusting in God's promises to her. Slowly Amy found that Jesus alone was enough for her.

Amy saw very few changes in Phil's life for many years. When I saw her not long ago, she told me that God had sent blessings and surprises to her that she could never have dreamed of. Amy and Phil had three children, and she told me that all of them are following the Lord. Phil has never openly committed his life to Christ, but he does attend church with her on occasion. She said, "I still pray for his salvation every day. I love him with all my heart and I know, even when I don't see any evidence of it, that God is working in Phil's life."

overbearing parents

WHAT YOU NEED TO KNOW

Adults who want to honor God still can get hung up on how to obey Him in relating to their parents. I am often asked, How do I honor my parents when I am past the age of dependence? Is obedience still an issue when I am self-supporting or married? My answer: An adult woman honors her parents by obeying and honoring God first.

A child's relationship with her parent has far-reaching implications. I have worked with women of all ages who struggle with how to relate to parents and in-laws who are controlling, possessive, demanding, or have unrealistic expectations that are not appropriate for mature relationships.

Adult children need to emotionally detach from their parents—to a certain degree—in order to become independent and healthy adults. Codependence is being enmeshed in another person's life to the point that you cannot separate your emotions from the other's emotions. It is an overinvolvement in another's life.

It is possible for an adult child and her parent to have a close, loving relationship that is tremendously rich and rewarding, even if they did not have one earlier. Encourage your counselees not to give up on that possibility, because God is able to do "exceeding abundantly above all that we ask or think" (Ephesians 3:20, KJV). Help her seek healing, if that is needed, while recognizing that her relationship with her parents may never be perfect.

A valuable resource for understanding and helping older parents is *Caring for Your Aging Parents* by Barbara Deane.

HELP AND HOPE FROM GOD'S WORD

Spend time reading and meditating on the following passages of Scripture, asking God to show you how you can use them to help someone who struggles with this issue.

Genesis 2:24
Matthew 19:4-6
Mark 7:9-13
Ephesians 6:1-3
1 Timothy 5:1-2,4

LANCE THE BOIL

When Lisa came to see me, she was very upset by her parents' accusations that she was not honoring them. When I asked her to tell me why they felt this way she told me her story.

Several months before, her husband, Ken, had accepted a job promotion. The position enabled them to buy a larger home and put their kids in a private school. The problem—at least according to Lisa's parents—was that the new job was in another state. Lisa's parents had adamantly opposed the move, and when Lisa and Ken disregarded her parents' wishes and moved anyway, her father stopped speaking to them and her mother cried every time Lisa called.

A few months after they moved, her mother called to tell her that they were selling their home and planning to join Ken and Lisa in their new location. Lisa told me that after her parents had moved, they constantly complained that Lisa and Ken did not include them in all their activities. They were around all the time and pouted if their grandkids didn't spend time with them instead of playing with their new friends. Lisa's father had begun to come to Ken's office for lunch every day. Sometimes he would burst into Ken's meetings to make a comment or suggestion. Their entire life revolved around their children and grandchildren. Ken and Lisa were feeling stifled and overwhelmed, and understandably so. They wanted a life of their own and a balanced relationship with her parents.

TAKE HER TO JESUS

Lisa's struggle with overbearing parents is not unusual, so I told her that she was not alone. I opened my Bible to Ephesians 6:1-3 and had her read "Children, obey your parents in the Lord, for this is right. HONOR YOUR FATHER AND MOTHER (which is the first commandment with a promise), SO THAT IT MAY BE WELL WITH YOU, AND THAT YOU MAY LIVE LONG ON THE EARTH."

I said, "Notice that the injunction in this passage is not just to obey your parents; it is to *honor* them. I believe this means that if it is not appropriate for adults to do as their parents say, we must still honor them."

According to Genesis 2:24, "For this reason a man shall leave his father and his mother, and be joined to his wife; and they shall become one flesh." Ken and Lisa had left their parents and joined together, but her parents were having trouble with that separation. I brainstormed with Lisa about how she could set some boundaries with her parents (see pages 127–128). I told her, "The challenge will be how you talk with your folks about having a separate life from you. First Timothy 5:1-2 has something to say about that: 'Do not sharply rebuke an older man, but rather appeal to him as a father, to the younger men as brothers, the older women as mothers, and the younger women as sisters, in all purity.'" I wanted to teach Lisa how to apply this verse to her situation, so I told her, "You and Ken need to go to your parents and appeal to them in a logical, loving way, regardless of what they say or do. An angry, argumentative spirit would be wrong. Communicate as best you can your love and appreciation for them. Express lovingly to them that you feel that everyone would be happier and healthier if you each had your separate lives. Tell them that you appreciate them and want them to be a part of your lives and that you would like to invite them to join you often. Make it clear that they are not to go to Ken's office unless specifically invited. Encourage your parents to join a Sunday school class at church and to make friends of their own. Your parents will be hurt. They are going to need time to face the truth of what you tell them."

When Ken and Lisa talked with her parents, they repeatedly assured her folks of their love and respect. Lisa cried because it was so difficult, knowing that her parents were hurt by their honesty. They tried to help her parents see that the children needed to play with their friends as well as spend time with Grandpa and Grandma. Even though Ken and Lisa were gentle and loving, her parents responded poorly, yelling, crying, and threatening.

Ken and Lisa struggled with anger at her folks for being so difficult and not making a life of their own. However, Lisa still chose to honor them. She did this by stopping by their house and calling them on the phone frequently, while maintaining firm boundaries with them.

One day Lisa called to tell me that she thought it might be easier to go back to the way it was before, because her parents were being so difficult. I said to her, "Your parents may hold this against you for a long time. But you need to proceed with your plan and maintain the boundaries you have set up while still treating them in a loving way. Be careful never to close any doors to the relationship or burn any bridges that cannot be repaired."

I told Lisa that her parents had probably been totally unaware that their world was so narrow. I challenged her to live according to Ephesians 4:32: "Be kind to one another, tender-hearted, forgiving each other, just as God in Christ also has forgiven you." Ken and Lisa were going to have to be especially kind and tenderhearted with her parents while they established a new model of relationship.

I said to her, "How you honor your parents is revealed not only in how you treat them but also in how you think and speak about them even when they are not around. Jesus said, 'Honor your father and mother,' and 'Anyone who speaks evil of father or mother must be put to death' (Matthew 15:4, NLT). Those strong words from the Old Testament law underline the importance of guarding our tongues with respect to our parents."

BELIEVE FOR HER

During another visit Lisa told me that her dad had begun to speak to her, but only when necessary. "I don't know if I'll ever have the relationship I used to have with my father," she cried. "He is so hard-headed."

As I handed her a tissue I said, "Lisa, if you keep your focus on your dad, you won't have any hope for his change. But remember, you walk with a God who is in the business of transforming people. I will stand with you in prayer for a restored relationship with your father, not because of who he is, but because of who God is."

HELP HER BECOME INDEPENDENTLY DEPENDENT

After the worst of the crisis, Lisa called me several times, wanting reassurance that she had done the right thing. "Should we have been so strong?" she asked.

"God joined you and Ken into a family," I responded. "His Word says that you are to leave your parents. Don't doubt it now; go forward, looking to Him. When you obey God's Word, you honor your parents at the same time. Let me pray for you: Heavenly Father, thank You that Lisa and Ken were able to talk with her folks and trust You for all the hard things that happened to them. We know that You will bless them because they were obedient. I pray for Lisa's parents that You will tenderize them and help them to grow through this experience. And Lord, bring down every wall that Satan has put up between these parents and their daughter, and restore a healthy bond of unity between them. In Jesus' name, amen."

A few months later, I walked into a restaurant and saw Lisa sitting at a table with her mother and father. She asked me to sit with them while I waited for my friend. Lisa said happily, "I invited my folks to lunch because they are leaving for a two-week cruise with some old classmates."

Later she told me that after many difficult months of remaining kind but firm, she was coming to a place of peace with her parents. "My folks are starting to have a few people in for dinner. They are finding new things to keep busy. And when we get together, we are beginning to have fun again. I have real hope that we can have the relationship that I long for. I really need them in my life."

pornography

WHAT YOU NEED TO KNOW

With the accessibility of the Internet, everyone with a computer at home is just a few keystrokes away from viewing millions of pornographic images without the embarrassment or risk of going out in public. As a result, pornography has become one of the most common problems that pastors and Christian counselors have to confront.

Consider these recent statistics about Internet pornography:

- Men admitting to accessing pornography at work—20%
- U.S. adults who regularly visit Internet pornography web sites—40 million
- PromiseKeepers men who said they had viewed pornography in the last week—53%
- Christians who said pornography is a major problem in the home—47%
- Adults admitting to Internet sexual addiction—10%

- Breakdown of male/female visitors to pornography sites—72% male and 28% female[1]

While the uninformed may view this problem as a matter of "boys being boys," it is not. Pornography is a serious addiction that most often originates in adolescence and then is brought into marriage. The addictive qualities of pornography will drive a person to seek greater and greater thrills that, if left unchecked, can lead to acting out in different forms, such as visiting strippers or prostitutes, engaging in affairs, inappropriate touching of children, and even incest.

The issues that cause a man to become involved in pornography are deep and painful, often rooted in childhood. Many men addicted to pornography have an intimacy disorder. When this is the case, the wife will be hurt even before she knows of the addiction, because she will sense the lack of intimacy in the marriage. When she learns of the pornography, she will feel threatened and fear that it will ruin their relationship. A man who is into pornography can lose his ardor for his wife. When this happens, he robs her of the exclusive relationship God intended between a man and woman. A woman will interpret her husband's involvement in pornography as rejection.

> **WOMEN AND PORNOGRAPHY**
>
> While pornography has largely been considered a problem that men face, be aware that more and more women are reporting that they struggle in this area.
>
> - Seventeen percent of all women struggle with pornography addiction.
> - Seventy percent of those women keep their cyber activities secret.
> - Women favor chat rooms two times more than men do.
> - One of three visitors to all adult websites are women. The number of women who access adult websites each month is 9.4 million.[2]

Wives in this situation will often be tormented with fears and questions such as, should I divorce him? Can I support my family? How and when will I tell the children? What will my friends and family think? As KTCs we can teach women to take every thought into captivity, to weigh carefully any advice people give to them, and to practice walking only in the light God gives. We need to counsel them to look to God about what to do; we need to help them think through the consequences of their actions so that they are prepared to accept what happens if God leads them to take action. We can remind them over and over that God will give wisdom for the next step. When a woman forgets this truth, she may take on a future that God does not intend for her.

It may be hard for a wife to believe, but her husband's addiction to pornography has very little to do with her. She will need to hear you say over and over that she is *not* the issue, nor is she responsible for her husband's sinful choices. She may feel that somehow she is not adequate and that is why her husband is doing this. It would be a mistake for her to think that she could compete with the unrealistic images that her husband has been looking at. A woman of any age can be devastated by the temptation to compare herself to the phantom women in her husband's life.

What else can you do to help a woman in this position? You can help her to face the truth of her circumstances. You can pray for her and with her and hold up her arms in faith. Find out what help there is in your area for those who struggle with addiction to pornography. Investigate accountability groups and other support structures for people struggling with addictions. Suggest counselees read the following books, or if you can afford it, have them on hand:

- *Wild at Heart* by John Eldredge
- *No Stones* by Marnie C. Feree
- *An Affair of the Mind* by Laurie Hall
- *Living with Your Husband's Secret Wars* by Marsha Means
- *False Intimacy* by Harry Schaumburg

Focus on the Family's website (www.family.org) also suggests many valuable resources.

Some churches are now tackling this issue and offer support groups for both women and men. Even if your counselee does not attend a church where something is available, she can go to another church's meetings or seek help through Al-Anon (a national program for family members of addicts).

Computer accountability programs for men and women, such as Covenant Eyes, can help hold people accountable for their computer activity (visit their website, www.covenanteyes.com).

Esther Ministries is specifically designed for women whose husbands have a problem with pornography. Their website, estherministries.org, can be a useful tool.

HELP AND HOPE FROM GOD'S WORD

Spend time reading and meditating on the following passages of Scripture, asking God to show you how you can use them to help someone who struggles with this issue.

2 Chronicles 6:30
Proverbs 4:23
Jeremiah 6:16; 23:24
Ezekiel 3:18-19
Nahum 1:7
Matthew 5:27-28
Ephesians 4:15; 5:1-4,11-15; 6:10-18
Philippians 4:7
James 1:5

LANCE THE BOIL

I met Jessica at a women's conference. She told me a sad story that I had heard many times before. Two years earlier, she had married a young man from her high school youth group. He came from a good Christian family and they had dated for three years before marrying. Jessica and her husband were helping out with the youth group, he occasionally taught the Bible study, and she was thinking things were going well between them. The week before the conference, while her husband was at work, she sat down at the computer to send a quick e-mail and discovered that he had been visiting pornographic websites. When she looked at the history on the computer, she realized that he had been doing this for quite some time. She was shocked, stunned, and sickened.

Jessica was nearly beside herself as she talked with me. She was afraid to leave her husband alone in their home. She didn't even feel free to go out to Bible study. She said, "I almost didn't come to the retreat this weekend because I am sure that when I am gone he feels he can do what he wants. But I was desperate to get away to figure out what to do."

She felt deeply hurt and completely bewildered by her husband's actions. She questioned whether she had ever satisfied him sexually or if she even could. "I am sharing him with other women that I can never compete with. I haven't talked to him about it because I don't know what to say. I am so mad. Will I ever be able to look him in the face and not feel disgusted and dirty? What can I do? What can I say?"

MEET HER FELT NEED

Like most wives of men who have an addiction to pornography, Jessica felt powerless and helpless. She needed to know that she was not and that God could give her wisdom about what to do—and the strength to do it.

I cried with Jessica, because I know there are no easy answers or pat solutions to the sticky mess of a pornography addiction. I said to her, "You are right to feel that you are sharing your husband with other women. Matthew 5:27-28 says, 'You have heard that it was said, "YOU SHALL NOT COMMIT ADULTERY"; but I say to you that everyone who looks at a woman with lust for her has already committed adultery with her in his heart.'

"Jessica, the first thing you need to do is confront your husband. Ephesians 5:11-15 says,

> Do not participate in the unfruitful deeds of darkness, but instead . . . expose them; for it is disgraceful even to speak of the things which are done by them in secret. But all things become visible when they are exposed by the light, for everything that becomes visible is light. . . .
>
> Therefore be careful how you walk, not as unwise men but as wise.

"You need to tell your husband that his addiction will ruin your marriage and that he must get help and change or there will be serious consequences. You must confront him with the fact that he is robbing you of his energy and love by his behavior. Nahum 1:7 says, 'The Lord is good, a stronghold in the day of trouble, and He knows those who take refuge in Him.' Believe this, Jessica! God will take care of you."

A woman who is dealing with her husband's pornography problem needs to seek God daily for strength and wisdom for the next step. According to James 1:5, God will give all the wisdom necessary, if we will simply ask. God knows her—and her husband—and if she can trust Him, He can begin to fill her with His peace: "And the peace of God, which surpasses all comprehension, will guard your hearts and your minds in Christ Jesus" (Philippians 4:7). I told Jessica, "God wants to guard your emotions and your thoughts and fill you with His peace, but you have to choose with your will to give everything over to Him."

In addition to confronting her husband, Jessica's immediate need was to lay down some boundaries with him. I talked with her about how she could make sure he understood that she would not tolerate the presence of pornography in their home. "Not only do you need to tell him this," I said, "you need to back up your words with actions."

Here are some things I suggested:

- Relocate the computer in a more visible area, such as the family room or kitchen.
- Download electronic guards onto the computer.
- Review the history of all website visits regularly. Although history can be deleted, a suggested family rule is that only a designated person can delete the history file. A deleted history by anyone other than the designated one is a sign of inappropriate use of the Internet.
- Make sure that televisions in the home can be seen by everyone; don't put one in a bedroom.
- Block certain television stations or have them eliminated from your cable package.

Just as alcohol has to be removed from the proximity of an alcoholic, steps must be taken to remove ready access to addictive, pornographic images.

Because pornography is so addictive, I warned Jessica that if she chose to keep watch over her husband's Internet activities, she should not go to any of the pornographic websites. The addresses themselves typically indicate the nature of the site.

I also encouraged Jessica to insist that her husband get professional psychological help from a godly counselor—immediately. Pornography is a cancer that will destroy. If a wife turns her head and ignores the circumstances, she is inviting destruction into her marriage. For that reason I said to her, "You are not responsible for your husband's sin, it is not your fault that he is doing this, but you *must* take steps to protect your marriage. You can tell him that you cannot trust him if he is not willing to get counsel. After a period of time, if you see that he is not making himself accountable to a godly man, let him know that you will call in your pastor or an elder to help him."

TAKE HER TO JESUS

While I didn't want Jessica to put her head in the sand, I knew that ultimately she had to put her husband in God's hands. I handed her my Bible and asked her to read 2 Chronicles 6:30 out loud to me: "Then hear from heaven Your dwelling place, and forgive, and render to each according to all his ways, whose heart You know for You alone know the hearts of the sons of men."

Then I asked her to read Jeremiah 23:24:

> "Can a man hide himself in hiding places
> So I do not see him?" declares the LORD.
> "Do I not fill the heavens and the earth?" declares the LORD.

When she finished reading, I said, "Both of those passages tell us that God knows your husband's heart. You are going to have to ask Him to let you know when you need to be especially aware of the temptations your husband is facing."

Then I prayed with Jessica and promised to continue to pray for them as a couple. "Dear Lord, Jessica has entered into a battle with the Enemy. We know that she is going to need Your special help through this time. Give her courage and strength. Help her to be forgiving, loving, understanding, and wise. Help them, as a couple, to see this battle to the end. And we trust You for deliverance. In Jesus' name, amen."

I knew that Jessica and her husband had many difficult days ahead, so I encouraged her to be still and listen to God's voice as best she could. I had no doubt that God is able to help Jessica not only survive this but also grow from it and experience the deep joy that comes from knowing that

God is worthy of trust. I wanted to give her a word picture of how God could redeem her situation, so I reminded her of the story of Achan.

Joshua 7 tells this very sad story concerning the Israelites' first battle after their victory at Jericho. They thought that the enemy was weak, so they didn't send many men into battle—and the enemy routed them. The Israelites were so frightened that their hearts "melted and became as water" (verse 5). When Joshua asked God why they had suffered defeat, God told him that there was sin in the camp. Eventually, God revealed that Achan's disobedience had been the cause. He had disobeyed God by hiding some goods he had stolen after one of Israel's victorious battles.

The Israelites then took Achan and everything that was his—his family, his cattle, and his goods (stolen and not stolen)—to the Valley of Achor, and stoned them and burned them. I am sure that when the Israelites thought of that place, they remembered their terrible defeat in battle and the heart-melting fear. Down through the generations, the Valley of Achor has meant trouble to God's people. That is why God's words in Hosea 2:15 are so precious to me, and I had Jessica read them: "There I will give her back her vineyards, and will make the Valley of Achor a door of hope. There she will sing as in the days of her youth, as in the day she came up out of Egypt" (NIV).

When she finished, I said, "In this verse God declares that in the place that reminded the children of Israel of their trouble, fear, and defeat, God promised to make a 'door of hope.' He can do the same for you. Even though your situation may seem devastating and the worst thing that could happen to you, your God is the God of hope. I want you to hold on to Him for what lies ahead.

"Your assurance is in God's promises to sustain you through everything He allows to touch your life. God can change your husband, if he will let Him. But don't put your hope in seeing your husband change; if you do, you might end up defeated. Put your hope in God and in the truth that He will be with you no matter what happens." When a woman walks with God, *she always has hope.* As KTCs we must believe this and help the counselee believe it as well.

At the end of the conference I said good-bye to Jessica and did not see her again until I was invited to speak at her church two years later. She came up to me after the meeting and told me that she had implemented my suggestions about the boundaries in their home. She and her husband were getting counseling and regularly attending church together. She said, "I have been living one day at a time and trying not to borrow the future. I fight fear a lot but am learning to trust God."

sexual abuse and rape

WHAT YOU NEED TO KNOW

Many women have experienced some sort of sexual abuse (incest, rape, or molestation). Note these sobering statistics:

- One in three girls is sexually abused before the age of eighteen. Of all physically or sexually abused girls, 53 percent say the abuse occurred at home, 65 percent say that it occurred more than once, and in 57 percent of the cases the abuser was a family member.[1]
- Victims of sexual abuse range in age from under two years to more than eighty years of age. Nearly half of rape cases are committed by people known to the victim.[2]
- Women and children are the most frequent victims of sexual abuse, but men can also suffer from it. Most sexual abusers are male, but there is a significant minority of female sexual abusers.[3]

As a biblical counselor, you can provide support and encouragement to a victim of abuse. Many times that support begins by getting your counselee the professional help she may need. Be sure to send a woman who has been sexually abused to a professional if she

- has an eating disorder
- is struggling with drug or alcohol addiction
- is suicidal
- is currently being abused
- is severely depressed

(For a more complete list, see pages 20–21.)

Professional counselors usually do not allow themselves to become engaged emotionally with their counselees. But a KTC can reflect the love of Jesus and His compassion to everyone she works with. Wounded people need to know that as a spiritual counselor you identify and hurt with them. (See chapter 6 to learn how to protect yourself from being overwhelmed by others' pain.)

The time needed for healing from sexual abuse varies from woman to woman. I have worked with some who have come to freedom from sexual abuse in one extended session. Others find healing after a much longer period of counseling, sometimes many years.

HELP AND HOPE FROM GOD'S WORD

Spend time reading and meditating on the following passages of Scripture, asking God to show you how you can use them to help someone who struggles with this issue.

Proverbs 5:22

Isaiah 43:18-19

Mark 7:14-23

Romans 12:19

1 Corinthians 6:15-18

1 John 1:9

LANCE THE BOIL

During our first meeting, Jen confided, "I have something to tell you that I've never told anyone before. A family member molested me when I was a child. It is keeping me from moving ahead in many areas of my life. Will you help me?"

Even though it would be painful for her, I knew that as a victim of sexual assault Jen needed to talk about the abuse, not leaving anything out, no matter how humiliating it was. So I asked her to tell me what had happened, how, when, and where it had taken place. This would be her first step toward healing. God could begin to work when she admitted her hurts.

Hearing the sordid details was not at all pleasant for me, nor were they easy for Jen to articulate, but her healing from the abuse depended on it. (In the case of a woman having symptoms but no memory of an incident of abuse, the KTC should not pressure her to come up with details because she could plant ideas in her counselee's mind. In my experience, I have dealt with several girls who were afraid they had been abused, and God showed them they had not. You can pray and sincerely ask God to reveal to your counselee if she has been abused. Be patient and trust God to show her in His time. If God does not make it clear, you have to conclude that she was not abused or that this is not His time.)

As Jen told me her story, I let her see my genuine sorrow and understanding for the pain. When she expressed her feelings harshly and used strong words, sometimes yelling, I was careful not to show shock or condemnation. It was not my place to correct her emotions, but to allow her to talk in a safe environment about how she felt.

When I was sure that Jen had expressed everything about the molestation, I told her that I was angry about what had happened to her, that I was grieved by what she had gone through. As a spiritual counselor, I represented Jesus to Jen. I reflected Him to her by saying, "God is angry too, and His heart is broken over your anguish."

When she finished telling me her story, I had her help me identify and write down the key points of her abuse so that we could both see what she had to process. That list would also serve as a guide for what we needed to focus on in our sessions.

I worked with Jen to help her articulate *how* she felt, because her feelings were as important to her healing as facing the truth of what happened. Jen felt that she was damaged and scarred, that the abuse had made her different from others. Like most victims of sexual abuse, she felt dirty and ashamed.

TAKE HER TO JESUS

I explained to Jen that what she was feeling was exactly what Satan wanted, that those emotions would keep her in bondage and prevent her from experiencing God's healing. "Satan would like to have you think that you are dirty—a second-class citizen. But that's not the way Jesus sees you. Let me show you what the Bible says about that." I wanted her to see and hear God's Word for herself so that she could clearly comprehend His truth. I opened my Bible to Mark 7:14-23 and had her read the passage out loud.

> After He called the crowd to Him again, He began saying to them, "Listen to Me, all of you, and understand: there is nothing outside the man which can defile him if it goes into him; but the things which proceed out of the man are what defile the man. If anyone has ears to hear, let him hear."

When he had left the crowd and entered the house, His disciples questioned Him about the parable. And He said to them, "Are you so lacking in understanding also? Do you not understand that whatever goes into the man from outside cannot defile him, because it does not go into his heart, but into his stomach, and is eliminated?" (Thus He declared all foods clean.) And He was saying, "That which proceeds out of the man, that is what defiles the man. For from within, out of the heart of men, proceed the evil thoughts, fornications, thefts, murders, adulteries, deeds of coveting and wickedness, as well as deceit, sensuality, envy, slander, pride and foolishness. All these evil things proceed from within and defile the man."

I then asked her the following questions. (Jen had been deeply hurt, so I made sure the tone of my voice and my attitude reflected the compassion in my heart for her—as a loving mother to her child.)

Who was made dirty when you were molested? Jen, like most victims, said that *she* was. I had her read the passage again until she could say to me, "The person who abused me was the one that was defiled."

She was surprised to realize that in God's eyes, the perpetrator of the abuse was made dirty (defiled), but that God viewed *her* as innocent and undefiled.

Careful not to belittle what had happened, I gently explained that she was hurt and violated, but *not* made dirty. I had to be specific: "Jesus said that nothing outside of you can defile you, not even when that man entered your body and touched you where he did. This act did not make you dirty, even if you experienced a sexual response (which would be normal), because your heart wasn't in it or you didn't understand what you were doing. This sin was done against you; it didn't come from you. It came from within the heart of an evil person. Who you are in your heart is what is important to God."

Then I gave Jen a visual image of how God sees her. "You are like a beautifully wrapped gift with a lovely diamond inside. When someone opens a box, they tear the paper and ribbon don't they? But that doesn't hurt the diamond. When God looks at you, He sees the beauty of the gem that you are."

Did the rapist/molester have evil thoughts when he did this to you? When I asked Jen this, she said, "Of course he did!"

I told her, "Your abuser definitely did have evil thoughts. Notice that verses 21 through 22 lists twelve items as evil things that come from within a person: evil thoughts, fornications, thefts, murders, adulteries, deeds of coveting and wickedness, deceit, sensuality, envy, slander, pride and foolishness. Eight or nine of them occurred in your situation." I wanted her to see how many things mentioned in the passage could have been part of his thinking.

Did your abuser take something of yours that he had no right to? When she said yes, I told her that was theft.

Could it be that the abuser caused your joy to die? I said, "Jen, if you do not choose to look at this incident from God's viewpoint, it will kill your joy."

Did this person deceive you in any way? When Jen nodded, I said, "You were deceived because you were introduced to the wrong kind of sensuality. There is a good kind of sensuality and a bad kind. The good kind is what is expressed in marriage, but what happened to you was wrong and it planted a lie in your heart about what the physical expression of love is."

Was he foolish to think he could get away with this? I said, "The Bible says that God will punish him (see Romans 12:19). God's punishment will be harsher than anything you could inflict on him. You can give that to God and leave it with Him."

My goal in asking these questions was to help Jen understand what had been done to her from a biblical perspective.

As Jen talked, I listened carefully for any expression of guilt on her part. Was she blaming herself for anything? When she said, "I shouldn't have gone with him. I didn't know that what we were doing would lead to this," I did not brush her feelings of guilt away with comforting words, because that would not give her relief. I knew that every person who has been violated experiences a sense of guilt, even if it is because she was in the wrong place or because she didn't have the strength or courage to stop what was going on. Jen, like many people, believed that if she could understand why the abuse happened, she could get peace in her heart. But because she could find no reasonable explanation, she assumed personal responsibility for what had happened to her.

Once we identified the areas where Jen felt guilty, I had her read 1 John 1:9 to me: "If we confess our sins, He is faithful and righteous to forgive us our sins and to cleanse us from all unrighteousness." I explained to her that even though she was not responsible for what the molester had done to her, in order to be free from the guilt that she was experiencing, she needed to be cleansed. Together we prayed a prayer based on that passage of Scripture.

After Jen prayed, she experienced only a degree of freedom and forgiveness. I told her that I believe this sometimes happens because sexual familiarity brings about a connection between the violator and the victim. Proverbs 5:22 talks about "the cords of . . . sin" that hold the wicked. That cord can also hold the one that was sinned against. I told her, "We can break this tie by understanding *all* of 1 John 1:9. Did you confess your part and did God forgive you? Because you do not feel free, look at the last line and read it again: And cleanses us from *all* unrighteousness. I believe that you were forgiven and cleansed from what *you* felt responsible for. Now let's ask God to cleanse you from what was *done* to you. God cleanses us from all unrighteousness, not just what we have done, but also what was done against us."

Jen prayed, "Lord, thank You for forgiving me of my guilt. I want to be completely free. Please wash me of all the horrible things that were done to me. Thank You for the promise that You will cleanse me from all the things that I have done as well as those evil things that were done to me."

When Jen was ready, I said to her, "Let's go back to the list that we wrote at the beginning. Are you ready to forgive your abuser and carry all these ugly things to the cross and lay them down? This is what forgiveness means. You give up your right to hold these things against the molester." I had Jen pray through the list, taking each thing, one by one to Jesus, forgiving and relinquishing her right to revenge, rebellion, and resentment. (See chapter 4 for more information about forgiveness.)

BELIEVE FOR HER

I wanted to help Jen clearly understand what God does for her, so I painted her a word picture. (I only give counselees word pictures that have a foundation in biblical truth.) I asked her to shut her eyes and imagine a crystal-clear pool of water, which represents the blood of Jesus. "Picture yourself walking into the pool up to your knees. In the middle is a fountain pouring out pure water. Walk under the spray. Now stand there so it streams down over your head and face. With your eyes closed, imagine that as the water flows over you, you are being washed in the clear, cleansing blood of Jesus."

Then I prayed this prayer for her: "Lord, wash everything in Jen, all her memories, so that when she remembers the abuse, it will not have a hold over her anymore. Bathe every dark corner of her mind. . . . Now, Father, saturate her eyes with your precious blood. She saw things that she should not have seen. . . . Lord, wash her ears so that she will be cleansed from the things that were said that were ugly and obscene. Purify her mouth. Now, Father, as that crystal-clear water pours over her body, over all the sacred parts of her, both inside and out, will You cleanse her from all the invisible marks of the sin that was done to her?"

When I finished praying, I had Jen keep her eyes closed and visualize herself stepping out of the pool and standing in a circle of light, dressed in a white dress. I instructed her to look up and imagine that God and Jesus were having a conversation about her. I said, "Jesus tells His Father, 'I went to the cross so that Jen could be pure and clean.' And God responds, 'I see her just as if she has never been touched by evil.'"

Then Jen and I turned to the list of all the things that she had released to forgiveness. Together we destroyed the paper. This symbolic act represented that the pain of the molestation was no longer hers to carry. I explained that because she had been cleansed from what was done to her, she could walk down the aisle at her wedding dressed in white. "You can present yourself to your new husband as pure, because that's how God sees you, and that is also how you can view yourself now that you have been washed clean.

HELP HER BECOME INDEPENDENTLY DEPENDENT

As we finished our time together I told Jen, "Now you have to choose whether you are going to believe that God is a good God. What was the purpose of this horrible thing? Why does He allow such things to happen to you?" I reminded her that God never promised that He would keep us from suffering, and I showed her examples from Scripture of what God's people suffered (see Hebrews 11:35-40).

Before we closed in prayer, I said, "Jen, you can be terrified and not be able to trust God all your life because of what you have gone through, or you can choose to walk with Him. You can stand on the truth that He is with you and rest in the fact that He wants only good for you, no matter how much it hurts. God's promise is that He will go through suffering with us. Your idea of happiness may be that you suffer no pain, but God wants to use your difficulties to conform you to the image of Jesus. Real happiness will be a by-product of His working in your life."

singleness

WHAT YOU NEED TO KNOW

Singleness can be very painful. A single woman may find herself yearning and grieving because she feels that she will always be alone. She may become desperate or give up on life and simply exist. If that happens, she will lose her sparkle and charm, which is the core of each woman's beauty. Or she may become bitter, tough, and indifferent, saying, "Men? Forget it! I don't need them."

A helpful resource for working with women who struggle with being single is *Sassy, Single and Satisfied: Secrets to Loving the Life You're Living* by Michelle McKinney Hammond.

HELP AND HOPE FROM GOD'S WORD

Spend time reading and meditating on the following passages of Scripture, asking God to show you how you can use them to help someone who struggles with this issue.

Jeremiah 2:13

Matthew 6:34

Luke 4:1-15

2 Corinthians 6:14-15; 10:5

LANCE THE BOIL

Tina was a lovely flight attendant whom I met at a conference. She told me that she was seeing someone, but that she didn't know if she should be. "I don't plan on marrying this man," she said. "I just enjoy the attention he gives me. Sometimes I wonder if I'll ever get married. At times I think maybe I should just marry him because I may never meet anyone else. I have tried to tell God that I am willing to be single all my life, but I'm not. I feel like there is a rift between God and me because I can't seem to do what I know He wants me to."

I responded, "Tina, I know life can be terribly lonely. I wasn't single for very long, but my husband traveled a great deal. He was gone 50 percent of the time, many times as long as three months at a stretch. When I felt overwhelmed by being alone, I had to tell the Lord that I needed Him to fill that loneliness with some special comfort. You can expect Him to help you through it. He will never ask you to do something that He will not enable you to do."

TAKE HER TO JESUS

As Tina told me her story, I identified several things that we needed to talk about. The first was her misconception about what she thought God wanted from her. "Tina, I believe that you are trying to do something God has not asked you to do. You imagine that you have to face being alone for the next fifty years. You seem to think, *I'll never have anyone to really love me or have a home and children.* God is not asking you to be willing to be single for the rest of your life; He is simply asking if you are willing to be single for one day—today. Matthew 6:34 says, 'Do not worry about tomorrow; for tomorrow will care for itself. Each day has enough trouble of its own.'

"You can be single for today can't you? The way to do that is to leave the future and all your tomorrows in God's hands."

I pointed out that Tina could make three choices that could help her trust God with her future.

- Take "every thought captive to the obedience of Christ," as Paul wrote in 2 Corinthians 10:5, instead of fretting about the future. She could lasso her thoughts and not let her mind go anywhere but to Him.
- Cultivate a love relationship with God, going to Him to meet all her emotional needs. I suggested to Tina that she do a project that could help her fall in love with Jesus (see "Falling in Love with Jesus" on page 87).
- Tell God upon awaking every morning, "I choose to be happily single for You today. I decide today to let You be my Sweetheart. I will dress for You, smile for You, and sparkle for You."

"If you make these choices every day," I concluded, "you will be able to celebrate life and be the beautiful, single woman God intends for you to be."

The second issue I addressed with Tina was her relationship with a nonbeliever. She needed to realize that when a woman seeks affection and attention wherever she can get it, feels sorry for herself, or resents her singleness, it can create a chink in her spiritual protection. A chink is a broken or cracked place in a woman's heart. Satan can then take advantage of that opening and come in like a flood, causing her to live a defeated life because her dreams are not coming true.

As I talked with Tina about this, I pointed her to Jeremiah 2:13, where God is talking to the Israelites about trying to meet their own needs and not looking to Him. God says,

> My people have committed two evils:
> They have forsaken Me,
> The fountain of living waters,
> To hew for themselves cisterns,
> Broken cisterns
> That can hold no water.

Then I said, "It is easy to go out and dig 'wells' to try to satisfy our own needs, such as spending time with men who aren't Christians. But going out with a non-Christian is like making broken wells that can hold no water. I want to give you a series of questions that can help you when you are trying to decide whether a relationship is worth pursuing, including the one you are currently in." (See "Should I Pursue This Relationship?" on page 203).

Tina looked at me sadly and asked, "What if I choose to live single for God each day? What does that mean about my sex drive and my need for physical affection? I can't deny that it is there." Her words identified the third issue that I wanted to address: her strong need for affection.

BELIEVE FOR HER

I answered, "You are absolutely right. And you're not the only one who struggles with that. We can find insight about what you can do about this in Luke 4:1-15, which gives the account of Jesus when He was severely tempted. We know that Jesus was divine, but He was also fully man, and He was hungry! He had not eaten for forty days."

I opened my Bible to verse 3, which tells us that the Devil encouraged

---

SHOULD I PURSUE THIS RELATIONSHIP?

Ask yourself these questions before pursuing a relationship.

- Has he invited Jesus to be his personal Savior and Lord?
- Does he build me up spiritually and emotionally?
- Do we constantly quarrel and bicker?
- Are we really compatible or just physically attracted to each other?
- Am I comfortable, at ease, and at peace about everything that is happening between us?
- Are our goals and priorities the same?
- How does he view authority, that is, parents, teachers, employer, police, and so on? (A spirit of rebellion will carry over into the relationship.)
- Is there any bitterness in him?
- Does he want a "mom" who pampers and babies him or a wife?
- How does he treat me in front of people? Is he proud and respectful of me?
- How does he treat me when we are alone?
- Does he respect my standards and the rules I've put on my life in such areas as touching, "making out," getting in on time, keeping my word, and so on?
- Does he have a good relationship with his family, especially his mother?
- Is he proud of my talents and abilities, or is he jealous and competitive?
- Does he dominate me or provide for me an atmosphere of freedom?
- Am I able to dominate him?
- Do I respect him?
- Is he hardworking and conscientious?
- How does he handle anger?
- Is he consistent and faithful in his walk with God with regard to involvement in the church, study of the Bible, sensitivity to the Holy Spirit on a daily basis? (If he is not faithful to God, he will not be faithful to his wife.)

Jesus to use His divine power to turn stones into bread. Then I said, "When hunger is referred to in Scripture, it represents all our basic drives and needs. Is there anything wrong with eating when you are hungry?"

"No, it is not wrong to eat," Tina replied.

"But turning stones to bread would have been the wrong use of Jesus' power, and He refused to do it. In the same way, there is nothing wrong with sex, but God has a sacred plan for it within the confines of marriage. To satisfy the sex drive is a basic human need. What you are feeling is normal and natural. I want you to see the principles here that can help you deal with your sexual desires."

Then I pointed out to her what happened when Jesus said no to Satan and to the temptations. First, Satan left Jesus and stopped the torment (see verse 13). Second, after Satan left Jesus, angels came and ministered to Him (see Matthew 4:11). Third, Jesus returned "in the power of the Spirit" (verse 14). Then He began ministering in that power (see verse 15).

"Tina, here is what this passage has to say about your situation. When you long for affection and are tempted to satisfy your sexual needs, you can choose to reject the temptation in Jesus' name and say no. And when you stand against that strong temptation and win, God will minister to your heart. I've talked with many women who have given in to the temptation of sex in order to satisfy that drive. Sadly, the power of God is gone from their life and the joy goes too. Yet when you choose to follow Jesus' example and don't seek to satisfy your physical needs in sinful ways, your relationship with God will become authentic and full of authority.

"I know the longing and temptation you are talking about. But I know the greater joy of choosing to channel that hunger into my walk with God. When God is my focus, He is free to minister to my heart and give me added power in ministry. You can say to Him, 'I love You more than my rights to having my needs met,' and you will know great blessing."

When my time with Tina drew to a close, I prayed this prayer for her: "Dear Lord, thank You for bringing Tina into my life. You know what the temptations are that she is struggling with. Help her to want to please You above all of her own desires. Help her to obey Your Word and recognize that if You did not withhold Jesus, will You not also, with Him, freely give her all things? Help her to know that those things You have planned for her will be right for her life. I pray she will trust You with all of her tomorrows. Amen."

spiritual strongholds

WHAT YOU NEED TO KNOW

As a KTC you will likely have some counselees who are in the grip of a spiritual stronghold. Paul wrote to the Ephesians, "For we are not fighting against people made of flesh and blood, but against the evil rulers and authorities of the unseen world, . . . and against wicked spirits in the heavenly realms" (6:12, NLT).

However, I want to caution you against seeing satanic oppression everywhere, as some are prone to do. Always try to address a counselee's problem by taking her to Jesus and encouraging her to apply God's Word to her situation. Pray with her and have her do any projects that may help her. If she does not experience freedom or deliverance after that, it may be that Satan has established a stronghold.

In *The Bondage Breaker*, Neil T. Anderson states,

I have learned from the Scriptures . . . *truth* is the liberating agent. The power of Satan is in the lie, and the power of the believer is in knowing the truth. . . . Persons in bondage are not liberated by what I do as the pastor/counselor, but what they do with my help. It's not what I believe that breaks the bonds, it's what *they* believe, confess, renounce and forgive.[1]

Jesus said, "I am the way, and the truth, and the life" (John 14:6). All truth comes from Him. That is why it is so important to bring the truth against Satan's lies. The challenge for the KTC is to help her counselee believe the truth, confess any sin that keeps her from intimacy with God, renounce that sin, and make sure she is walking in forgiveness.

Some of the best helps for dealing with spiritual strongholds are books by Neil T. Anderson, such as *The Bondage Breaker* and *Victory over the Darkness.*

HELP AND HOPE FROM GOD'S WORD

Spend time reading and meditating on the following passages of Scripture, asking God to show you how you can use them to help someone who struggles with this issue.

2 Chronicles 16:9

Job 1:12

Psalm 91:4

Matthew 16:19; 18:18-20

Luke 10:17-19

Romans 8:26-27; 13:12; 16:20

2 Corinthians 6:7; 10:4; 11:14

Ephesians 1:19-20; 6:10-19

2 Timothy 2:26

Hebrews 7:25

James 4:7

1 Peter 5:8-10

1 John 4:4

Revelation 12:10-11

LANCE THE BOIL

Pam called from another city and said she needed to talk. She told me she was so desperate that she was willing to drive several hours to see me. When she arrived, she sank down in a chair, put her face in her hands, and cried, "I don't know if I can tell you this; I am so ashamed."

"Pam, there is nothing you can tell me that will shock me. I want to know what is on your heart."

After she composed herself a bit, she said, "I have been a Christian since I was a little girl. I have always had my heart set on going into some kind of full-time service. A little over a year ago, I felt that I needed to get some experience in the business world, so I took a job as executive assistant to the young operations manager of a large corporation in my town. He was not married, but he was living with his girlfriend. I really enjoyed the job and loved working for him. Many times we had to work late to meet deadlines, and he started taking me out to eat when we finished. I wasn't really aware of how it happened, but pretty soon I realized that my heart was getting entangled.

"One night after going out for dinner, we were in the middle of a fascinating discussion, so I invited him into my apartment to finish the conversation. One thing led to another and we ended up in bed. I've been sleeping with him for about three months now, and he tells me he loves me, but he's still living with his girlfriend. I am miserable. I know that God isn't pleased with what I have been doing, and my soul is dark. I feel so desperate. It's all such a mess. I have got to get away from this man. I seem to have no strength to say no when I am with him.

"I have made some calls, and a friend of mine here in Portland has offered to let me live with her until I can find another job and get my own place. I am going back home to quit my job, and I hope to move here in just a few days. If I don't get away soon, I don't know if I ever will. When I move here, will you meet with me and help me get back on track with God?"

MEET HER FELT NEED

I told Pam that I would be happy to meet with her when she moved. But I also told her, "Before you go back, I want to talk with you about several things. First of all, you have confessed to me what has happened, but have you confessed it to God and made it right with Him? Have you told Him that you have gone against His way?"

When she nodded, I continued, "You are wise to realize that you have to get away from the situation. But it will be very hard to quit your job and say good-bye to your boss and break those ties. Still, God can give you the strength you need." I reminded her that "the eyes of the LORD move to and fro throughout the earth that He may *strongly support those whose heart is completely His*" (2 Chronicles 16:9, emphasis mine). We prayed together, and Pam left to quit her job and move back to Portland.

TAKE HER TO JESUS

It wasn't long before Pam called to say that she was back in town. When she came to see me she looked thin and haggard; her voice and demeanor conveyed sadness. She told me, "A part of me knows I did the right thing, but I can't get this guy out of my mind. I asked God for forgiveness and have done everything I know to get back on track, but something is not right. My spirit is so heavy."

"Pam, do you know what a stronghold is?" I asked her. "The dictionary says it is a well-fortified place, a fortress, a place that serves as the center; or it is being of certain opinions or attitudes. When there is a vulnerable spot in the spiritual armor of a Christian, Satan can build a stronghold. When a believer willingly and repeatedly participates in an area of sin, she yields occupation rights to the Enemy in that area. Once he takes over, he does not want to leave, and the believer is in bondage.

"I believe this may have happened to you. You have asked God for forgiveness, but you may need to do further spiritual work because of the ground that the Enemy gained through your disobedience. Are you willing to work on that? Would you join me in warfare prayer against Satan and the oppression he has placed you under?"

Pam said, "I am willing to do anything to be free of this awful heaviness. I want to be right with God."

I asked Pam to read Luke 10:17-19 aloud to me:

The seventy returned with joy, saying, "Lord, even the demons are subject to us in Your name." And He said to them, "I was watching Satan fall from heaven like lightning. Behold, I have given you authority to tread on serpents and scorpions, and over all the power of the enemy, and nothing will injure you."

I said, "The Lord gave the disciples power over demons, and this promise is for all believers. The disciples came back after experiencing supernatural power when they ministered in Jesus' name. Jesus rejoiced with them.

"In this passage, the demons appear as serpents and scorpions. However, strongholds and demonic activities do not always appear ugly. According to 2 Corinthians 11:14, Satan can come as an "angel of light." Many strongholds come through relationships that may seem beautiful to the participant, just as yours did in the beginning. The Bible says that the authority Christ gives is over *all* the power of the Enemy, whether ugly or beautiful. The Scripture says not to be afraid, because nothing can injure those who are in

Christ. We have nothing to fear, but we must be prepared for battle."

I took my Bible from Pam and opened it to Ephesians 6 and began reading at verse 10: "'Be strong in the Lord and in the strength of His might. Put on the full armor of God, so that you will be able to stand firm against the schemes of the devil.' This verse tells us that we carry God's strength with us when we go into battle against the Enemy. We are also supposed to put on the full armor of God when we do battle with him, but in order to do so, we need to be clean before God. We must confess any sin that we know about. Let's examine our hearts for sin and prepare for spiritual battle by praying silently for cleansing."

After a few moments of silent prayer, during which I made sure my own heart was right before God, I went on. "Ephesians 6:18 tells us that a part of the armor is prayer. Pam, I am going to cover us with a prayer of protection. Dear Lord, we thank You for the blood of Jesus Christ shed on Calvary for victory over the Enemy. I pray for protection for Pam, her family, and everything that pertains to her. I pray also for myself, my family, and everything that pertains to me. Thank You for the promise in Ephesians 1:19-20 that the very power that raised Jesus from the dead is available to we who believe. In that power we pray, amen."

Because I know that Satan takes special advantage of a believer when there has been sexual immorality, I began praying against the strongholds he might have set up in that area of Pam's life. I asked her to name and renounce anything that was holding her in bondage. Then I prayed, naming and binding in the name of the Lord Jesus Christ, by the blood shed on Calvary, all the sin entrenched in her life that she had confessed to me. I prayed against the control this man had over her, about her feelings of helplessness, and about the power of her sexual drive. We named and bound everything Pam felt was holding her in bondage. Then we asked Jesus Christ to take away everything that we had spoken of and anything else that was not of His Spirit. We asked that the demonic, oppressive spirits would go and not return.

I then asked the Holy Spirit to fill her clean heart with His light, His peace, and His very presence. I prayed, "Lord, according to Your promise, we stand on the fact that You have cleansed these things from Pam's life. Now I release in her heart and life all the fruit of Your Spirit: love, joy, peace, patience, kindness, goodness, faithfulness, gentleness, self-control" (Galatians 5:22-23).

HELP HER BECOME INDEPENDENTLY DEPENDENT

When we finished praying, I explained to Pam that she could stand on the promise of God and accept by faith that the evil forces were now gone. "However," I said, "Satan will try to send fresh recruits in those very areas of struggle. One way he will try to come against you is through the things this man gave to you. Get rid of everything that would remind you of him—all the letters, pictures, and gifts of any kind, even if they are valuable. The meaning infused in those items can have a strong hold on you. They represent something you have put behind you. If you cannot bring yourself to get rid of them, bring them to me and I will do it for you."

I encouraged her to stand firm in God and not give in to the temptation to think about her boss or to get back in touch with him, even if he tried to contact her. I said, "If you are struggling, call me for prayer so we can stand together against the Enemy." I reminded her that if she could not reach me, that meant God intended for her to rely on Him alone to help her resist the Enemy. I assured her that the Holy Spirit and Jesus were both interceding for her (see Romans 8:26-27; Hebrews 7:25) and that she didn't need me.

The next time Pam came to see me, she had several shopping bags of things that her former boss had given her, including clothes, some jewelry, letters, cards, and pictures. She held them out and said, "I couldn't bring myself to get rid of all this stuff. Will you do it for me?" We prayed together over the bags, and I disposed of them after she left.

I was in touch with Pam for a few months and then didn't hear from her for several years. Not long ago she called me. She told me that she was happily married and teaching a women's Bible study in her church. A young woman in her group was in a situation similar to the one she had been in. Pam asked me to explain again the principles that I had used with her so that she could help that young woman gain freedom from the bondage she was in. What a blessing to learn that Pam is living in victory and serving Jesus to help other women!

suicide

WHAT YOU NEED TO KNOW

A KTC *must not* take the potential of suicide lightly. Consider these statistics about this growing problem:

- In the past forty-five years, suicide rates have increased by 60 percent worldwide. Suicide is now one of the three leading causes of death among those aged fifteen to forty-four (both sexes). There are up to twenty times more attempts than completed suicides.[1]
- Suicide is the eighth leading cause of death for all Americans and is the third leading cause of death for young people aged fifteen to twenty-four.
- Males are four times more likely to die from suicide than females. But more females attempt suicide than males.
- Each suicide intimately affects at least six other people.
- Suicidal behavior is not inherited, but the risk may be higher for those who have lost a close relative or loved one to suicide.

- Most suicidal people communicate their intent to kill themselves before they attempt to do so.[2]

In *How Can I Help?* Lynda Elliott states that "a sudden, strong shift from depression into euphoria can be a signal that someone has decided how and when to die."[3] If a woman you are meeting with expresses any suicidal thoughts, *send her to a professional counselor.* You may need to go with her to ensure that she follows through on the appointment. If going to a professional presents a financial hardship for her, alert family members or her church to your concern and solicit financial help for her. Consider carefully whether she needs to be put on some sort of suicide watch.

HELP AND HOPE FROM GOD'S WORD

Spend time reading and meditating on the following passages of Scripture, asking God to show you how you can use them to help someone who struggles with this issue.

Psalm 139

Romans 8:1,31-39

1 Corinthians 3:16-17; 10:10

Hebrews 9:27

James 4:7

LANCE THE BOIL

Anne came to me with a boyfriend problem. After several sessions, I thought we had successfully worked through her issues. She was a lovely girl, a dedicated Christian who dreamed of being a pastor's wife. I suggested some steps she could take, and she agreed to follow through on what I asked of her. One evening after meeting with Anne, I got a call saying that she had attempted suicide. I was devastated and frightened because I had no idea that she had been thinking of taking her life.

After our session, Anne had gone back to her apartment, swallowed a bottle of pills, and called her mother. They talked for half an hour. Even though she was talking to her mom, Anne never let on what she had done. When she hung up, she went to bed, planning to fall asleep and never wake up. Later, for some reason, Anne got up to go to the bathroom. One of her roommates saw her stumbling down the hall and knew something was wrong. She called for help. They got Anne to the hospital and saved her life.

When Anne came to see me the next week, I asked her to forgive me for not meeting her needs and for not recognizing her desperation. I asked, "Were you thinking, *The world would be better without me* or *It would be easier to end it all*?"

Anne thought for a bit and said, "Yes, I have been saying that to myself."

I replied, "I am sorry. I should have asked if you were having destructive thoughts. I was afraid it would jeopardize the rapport we were building, and I didn't want you to think I doubted your commitment to Christ."

I asked Anne to tell me what happened at the hospital. When she told me that she was required to have professional counseling, I said, "I think that is excellent. If you would like, you can meet with me after your sessions with him in order to process what he is telling you. I can help you work through what he asks you to do and hold you accountable. I will be praying for your meetings with the psychologist."

BELIEVE FOR HER

I told Anne how thankful I was that God had spared her life. "You are such a precious girl. You have family and friends who love you. It would have devastated me and so many others if you had succeeded in taking your life. Most of all, you are God's beloved child, precious to Him. He knows you better than you know yourself. You know that Psalm 139:15 says that He was there when you were formed in secret. His thoughts for you outnumber the sand. I pray that you will never again lose sight of His profound love for you and that it will always hold you to a high standard."

TAKE HER TO JESUS

"Anne," I asked, "do you know where those destructive thoughts came from? They *did not* come from your own mind. Satan was sitting on your shoulder and whispering into your ear. First Corinthians 10:10 calls Satan 'the destroyer.' He tries to destroy believers. He cannot take away salvation or destroy the soul, but if he can get someone to take her life, God's plan for that person is thwarted, giving Satan a victory. Satan is trying to cross God's purposes in our lives.

"I can tell by the look on your face that you are thinking that people are making way too big a deal over this. But you need to realize that attempted suicide is very serious. Right now you are feeling all right and you can assure everyone that you won't try to take your life again, but what about when you feel despair and discouragement? If those ideas ever come to you again, I want you to remember you have access to power to deal with the destroyer."

I wanted to teach Anne how to access God's power, so I said, "James 4:7 tells us, 'Submit therefore to God. Resist the devil and he will flee from you.' You can resist Satan by acknowledging out loud, 'I know where this idea is coming from, and I reject it in Jesus' name.' Or 'I know you're the great destroyer and I don't want to have anything to do with you! Get away from me, in the name of the Lord Jesus Christ!'"

When we turn the searchlight of God's Word on the Enemy, it diminishes him. A believer can stand on the truth of what God declares in Scripture. For example, Romans 8:1,31-34:

Therefore there is now no condemnation for those who are in
Christ Jesus. . . . What then shall we say to these things? If God
is for us, who is against us? He who did not spare His own Son,
but delivered Him over for us all, how will He not also with Him
freely give us all things? Who will bring a charge against God's
elect? God is the one who justifies; who is the one who con-
demns? Christ Jesus is He who died, yes, rather who was raised,
who is at the right hand of God, who also intercedes for us.

"Anne, Satan spoke condemning words to you and you acted on
them. But God tells you that there is no condemnation for you because
you are in Him. I want you to turn the power of another truth on in your
heart by affirming out loud." Then I had her read Romans 8:35,37-39:

Who will separate us from the love of Christ? Will tribulation,
or distress, or persecution, or famine, or nakedness, or peril, or
sword? . . . But in all these things we overwhelmingly conquer
through Him who loved us. For I am convinced that neither
death, nor life, nor angels, nor principalities, nor things present, nor things to come, nor powers, nor height, nor depth,
nor any other created thing, will be able to separate us from the
love of God, which is in Christ Jesus our Lord.

I told Anne to use these verses as a reminder that not even the most
miserable thing happening in her life could cut her off from God's
love.

Many experts encourage counselors to ask their counselees who
are suicidal to sign a contract, and that is what I did with Anne. I told
her that it would help her to process what her options are if she is ever
tempted to think of suicide again and that it was a way of helping me
hold her accountable (see "No Injury Contract" on page 218).

No Injury Contract

1. I commit not to injure myself in any way, because . . . *

2. If I have thoughts about injuring myself, I will attempt to do the following things:

3. If these things do not work and I continue to have thoughts about injuring myself, I will:

Counselee's Signature _____

Counselor's Signature_____

Date _____

* If your counselee has trouble filling out this contract, here are some examples of how she might answer.

For question 1:
- It would devastate my family.
- It would upset my friends.
- It would disappoint God.
- It would ruin God's plan for my future, and I would have to answer to Him for it.
- If I survived, I could be damaged or handicapped for the rest of my life.
- If I survived, I would have to live with the shame and embarrassment of gossip.
- Someone would find me, and they would never get over it.

For question 2:
- Talk to a friend.
- Eat something.
- Get some exercise.
- Ask for help from a counselor.
- Listen to upbeat music.
- Read.

For question 3:
- Call a suicide hotline.
- Call 911.
- Go to the emergency room.

BELIEVE FOR HER

I gave Anne a few minutes to fill out the contract. As she wrote, I prayed silently, *Dear Father, I want to praise You for sparing Anne's life. I know that You have wonderful plans ahead for her. I pray against every dark spirit that would come to discourage Anne from living the life that You have for her. Help her to become stronger than ever as a result of this incident. And may she live and shine and serve You with all of her being. Use her to help many other discouraged young women. Thank You that You use the things that You teach us to help others. In Jesus' name, amen.*

When Anne finished, we went over her answers together. At several points I made suggestions about things that she could add to make her answers more complete. When we finished reviewing the document, Anne and I signed it solemnly. I made a copy and gave her the original, making sure she knew I was keeping the copy myself.

Anne saw the psychologist for several months. After each session with him, she and I talked about what she had learned that week. In our conversations I sought to confirm the truth that she was hearing from the psychologist, to support her in her determinations to apply his suggestions, and to praise her in every way I could.

In looking back over what happened, Anne told me, "In spite of the embarrassment and the turmoil I caused, I am almost glad that this whole thing happened, because I have come to know myself and God better."

worth

WHAT YOU NEED TO KNOW

Despite a multitude of counselors, self-improvement books, and seminars, many people today question their value. Because many self-worth issues are rooted in unhappy experiences from childhood—cruel words from family members or mistreatment from significant adults—even those we might least expect can struggle with feelings of inadequacy and low self-worth.

This problem is not new. It has been around as long as people have been on this earth. Eighty-year-old Moses grappled with this issue when God asked him to lead the Israelites out of slavery. Even though he had been handpicked by God to do this special job, Moses didn't feel he was up to the task. He kept asking God, "Who am I to do this?" (Exodus 3:11, my paraphrase).

If I had been God, I would have said to Moses, "Look how I prepared you and trained you all these years, look at the background I gave you. You can do the job." But God said only two things to Moses: "I am God, and I will certainly be with you" (verse 12, my paraphrase).

I have observed that the issue of self-worth needs to be addressed several times throughout one's life. Each phase or season of life brings new factors into play, and we must settle the issue of our worth all over again in light of the changes that have occurred in us.

Some Christians think that a longing for self-worth is wrong, but it's not. In *The Search for Significance*, Robert McGee writes, "We must understand that this hunger for self-worth is God-given and can only be satisfied in Him."[1] God planted in each of us a desire to be accepted, loved, and appreciated.

Our job as KTCs is not to reprimand our counselees for having this desire. Instead it is to help them know how to go about satisfying that desire in a godly way. To teach them to put their focus on God rather than on themselves. To turn their eyes upward rather than inward.

Most women who are unhappy will confess that they have a poor self-image. This struggle automatically takes their focus off God and onto themselves, which is Satan's goal. When a woman can stand on who God is, she can come to a whole new appreciation of herself, regardless of felt limitations.

Some great resources for understanding who God has made us to be and how we can best serve Him are *Live Your Calling: A Practical Guide to Finding and Fulfilling Your Mission in Life*, by Kevin and Kay Marie Brennfleck, and *Victory over the Darkness: Realizing the Power of Your Identity in Christ*, by Neil T. Anderson.

HELP AND HOPE FROM GOD'S WORD

Spend time reading and meditating on the following passages of Scripture, asking God to show you how you can use them to help someone who struggles with this issue.

Psalms 27:10; 139:13-16

Isaiah 43:7; 45:9-12

Romans 8:28-29; 9:20-21
1 Corinthians 1:7; 12:7-11,18
2 Corinthians 10:12
Galatians 5:22-23
Philippians 1:6,20

LANCE THE BOIL

Karina came to see me for help with her deep need for love and acceptance, an issue she said she had struggled with for many years. She told me that she was full of insecurities, self-doubt, and dislike for herself, saying, "I want to get this straightened out before I get married and have a family."

When I asked her to tell me what she believed was behind her feelings, she said she had never felt that her parents loved her. She told me, "It was as if there was something between us that I could never put my finger on. When I got to graduate school and took a psychology class, I realized I needed to find out if there was anything to the rejection I felt. I went home over a long weekend, determined to discover if it was just in my head.

"One night I asked my mother what was going on in her life when she was pregnant with me. She was silent for a while, then she told me my father hadn't wanted another child and was upset over the pregnancy—so much so that my parents were separated most of the time when Mom was carrying me. She told me that my dad didn't even come to the hospital when I was born. When I was just a few days old, she sent me to live with a cousin of hers because she was so upset and overwhelmed by trying to take care of my brother and sister alone. When she and my dad finally reconciled two years later, they brought me home. My mother told me that for years when she looked at me, I reminded her of that miserable time in their marriage."

Karina looked at me dry-eyed, but I could see hurt in her eyes. She continued, "It was a revealing moment for me. As a baby I did not bond with my parents. Then, when they did take me home, I represented a painful time in their lives. I have always felt on some level that they didn't want me or love me in the way they loved my brother and sister.

"My mother says that she and Dad really did love me. And I believe it in my head, but my heart is hurt from all those years of sensing that rejection and lack of bonding. Even though I know what happened when I was little, I still have incredible waves of feeling inadequate. There are times when I think, *Why would anyone want to be my friend?* or *Why did I think I could do this?* I doubt myself and my abilities all the time. How can I move ahead in life with all these strikes against me?"

My eyes were full of tears. Even though I hear many painful stories, I always ask God to keep my heart tender to the suffering of each person He brings into my life. I said, "Karina, I am so sorry for what you have suffered. You sensed something that turned out to be true. Some people feel those things and never find a reason for it. Whether or not a person has a reason for what they feel, the Bible addresses what God wants to do in us with our self-doubt."

Karina needed to take several steps to experience healing from the deep wounds that had caused her feelings of worthlessness: (1) forgive her parents, (2) reject the negative thought patterns that had taken hold of her mind as a result of her childhood pain, (3) replace those thoughts with God's perspective on who she is in His eyes, and (4) act on that truth.

TAKE HER TO JESUS

To teach her how she could do those four challenging things, I took Karina to Jesus. I opened my Bible to Romans 8:28-29 and reminded her that her upbringing was a part of God's plan to mold and shape her—and so were any present or future environments.

I went on to say, "He promises to work everything together for your good. You can choose to be hindered by your background and heredity, or decide to accept them and cooperate with God in the wonderful plan He has for you. I believe that to address our need for love and acceptance, we must first forgive those who have wounded us. Have you forgiven your parents for their rejection and the painful things you learned when you were home?"

Karina answered, "I have been doing a lot of forgiveness work since my visit home. My parents couldn't have realized how deeply I would be affected by what was going on between them. I can say that I really have given that to God."

Because Karina was a mature believer, she knew how to forgive and what the Bible says about it. If she had not understood the importance of forgiveness, that is where I would have started.

LIFE STEPPING-STONES

1. Write out each "stepping-stone" or key moment in your life. For example, some of my stepping-stones are:

   - born in China
   - returned to United States at six
   - found Christ at eight
   - spent a year in bed at nine because of tuberculosis
   - moved to Indiana
   - at thirteen, committed my life for ministry
   - met Norman

2. Mark an X beside those points which were out of your control
3. Put a + beside those which were a matter of your choice.
4. Be prepared to share what you have written.

At the end of our time together, I asked her to do the "Life Stepping-Stones" project (above) and told her that we would go over it during her next visit. I assigned her this project to get to know her better and to identify points of pain that we might need to deal with. My goal was to help her identify what had happened to her that she had no control over as well as what things were her choice. Karina needed to see clearly which steps she had taken because of her own choices, as most of us want to blame others rather than take responsibility for our own contribution to our problems. She also needed to see *and accept* that the things over which she had no control had come to her through God's hand. I let her know that the project would likely take a minimum of two hours, and I encouraged her to set aside the time needed to complete it before our next session.

The following week, when I asked her if she had done the project, Karina replied that she had. I had her share her stepping-stones with me and tell me which things had happened because of her own choices and which had been beyond her control. As she went through each stepping-stone, I watched her body language and listened for the emotions she expressed. A quivering lip, teary eyes, clenched fist, and other body language may reveal feelings and events a counselee may have trouble talking about. Those are a signal to me that I need to probe more deeply.

MEET HER FELT NEED

The damage to Karina's sense of herself had been deepening for many years and would continue if she did not replace her thoughts with God's perspective. I said, "Karina, I want you to put God's truth alongside the painful things that have been said and done to you. One way to do that is to read and memorize Scripture. You need to reprogram the messages that you believed when you thought that you were not lovable or valuable. To help you identify those things, I want you to do a project on self-acceptance" (see page 227).

When Karina returned with the project completed, we reviewed her answers. Then I said, "Many Bible passages address what you are struggling with." I asked her to write down the following biblical promises:

- Psalm 139:13-16 says that God created you and was there when you were formed.
- Isaiah 43:7 reveals what God made you for.
- Romans 8:29 gives you His goal for your life.
- Psalm 27:10 affirms God's involvement in your life.
- 1 Corinthians 12:7,18 says God has designed you for specific achievements, giving you a special function in the body of Christ.
- Romans 9:20-21 challenges the questions you ask about the way you were made.
- Isaiah 45:9-12 dares you not to question what He does and who He is.
- Philippians 1:6 says that God is not finished with you.

SELF-ACCEPTANCE

1. List the things about yourself that you do not like in these two areas:
   a. *Your past circumstances:* your background and the influences that have shaped you. For example, your parents, family, or "bad breaks," such as illnesses, losses, mistakes, and limited opportunities.
   b. *Who you are in the present.* Your personality, appearance, abilities, skills, and status.
2. Write out what happened to you in the past that was good as well as what you like about yourself now.
3. Go through the entire list, both negative and positive, and mark which things you can work on to bring about change. What are the things that cannot be changed? Are you willing to face and accept them and then lay them at the cross?

"Karina, God is working to make you all that He has in mind for you to be. He does not expect you to be a finished product now. If you are seeking to cooperate with Him, your disappointment in your flaws and failures can be a reminder that He will not stop the work He has begun until He has conformed you to the very attractive image of Jesus. You will only be perfect when you see Him face-to-face."

I encouraged Karina to select one of the verses and memorize it. "By keeping God's Word in front of your eyes, you can more easily discipline your heart and mind to reject the negative thoughts about yourself and affirm the truth that you have placed there instead. I have cards with verses on them over my dryer, in front of the kitchen sink, and on the mirror where I put my makeup on. It is a way to keep reminding myself of the truth that I want to get down into my heart."

BELIEVE FOR HER

Karina had experienced rejection from her parents. Even though she had dealt with their rejection, those wounds would take time to heal. She needed me to continually affirm to her the truth that she is beloved of God, just as she is right now. To encourage her to walk in the truth of who she is in God's eyes, I told Karina about my friend Miss Jenny.

Miss Jenny was ninety years old and nearly deaf. She attended the first church Norman and I pastored, arriving each week in a wheelchair. One Sunday I leaned down and shouted into her ear, "Miss Jenny, do you know God loves you?" She looked at me as if I had lost my mind and yelled back, "Of course He does. I am His special child!" Her response surprised me because outwardly she didn't have many reasons to believe that she was special. After all, she was old, deaf, and couldn't walk. But she had come to believe the truth of her value in God's eyes by getting to know her Creator, accepting her limitations, and appreciating how special she was to Him.

Miss Jenny had come to an understanding of her worth in God's eyes because she had gotten to know Him. That was where Karina needed to start. I asked her to do a project that would help her understand who God is (see "Who God Is" on page 229) and to be prepared to share it with me during our next visit. I assigned Karina this project with several objectives in mind. One was for her to learn how to look at Scripture and mine the riches of God's character from it. The other was to help her find an aspect of God that she could hang on to in her everyday life.

HELP HER BECOME INDEPENDENTLY DEPENDENT

Karina came for her last visit with me. She was about to receive her graduate degree and would be moving away soon. I wanted to prepare her for what was ahead so that she would not get discouraged or sidetracked, so I said, "Karina, you have grown much this past year. You have learned how to replace the lies you grew up believing about yourself with the truth of what God says about you. I have seen you express a new confidence in your approach to people, you have taken leadership here at school, and you are open to receiving affection and giving it to others.

> **WHO GOD IS**
> 1. Read Psalms 145–147.
> 2. Make a list of everything it says about who God is and what He does.
> 3. Pray through the list.
> 4. Ask God which aspect or characteristic of Himself He wants you to stand on for today. Read over the list daily for a period of time and claim different facets of God's character for your struggles.

"However, you should be aware that there will be times when the issue of your value and worth will come up again. Every time your circumstances change or become difficult, the temptation will be to fall back into your old patterns of thinking. Do you remember the process we went through when we began to meet together to work on your feelings of rejection?

"First, I asked you if you had forgiven your parents, who had played such a painful role in your feelings about yourself. Forgiveness work is something that you will have to do whenever painful things arise in your life. Then I encouraged you to reject those negative thoughts and replace them with truth from God's Word. When you struggle with your self-worth, review the verses you have memorized and find others to add to your arsenal. Finally, you must choose to walk and live as the beloved child of God that you are, just as Miss Jenny did.

"What gives me a sense of value is remembering that because Christ lives in me, when I walk into a room, His Holy Spirit comes with me. When I am seated on an airplane or talking with someone, the Lord is also there because He is in me. To help you remember that, I'd like to encourage you to study the Bible, looking for verses that tell you who God says you are because of your union with Him. Make a list of those verses that you can stand on for His perspective on your worth."

As Karina left my office for the last time, I did what I always do after a counselee leaves my office: I entrusted her to God.

for the ktc in training

QUESTIONS FOR STUDY AND DISCUSSION

Write out your answers to these questions and come to the training session prepared to share what you have written.

Chapter 1: "I Need Help! Can I Talk with You?"

1. Describe your spiritual journey in no less than five paragraphs.
2. List several reasons why you would like to learn more about Kitchen Table Counseling.
3. Describe what you hope to impart to the women you counsel. What do you think are the greatest needs of the women you know?
4. What do you do to cultivate your walk with God? What would you like to add to it? Make a specific plan to add it. Include in your plan what you want to do as well as when and how you will make it happen.

Chapter 2: "Am I Really Qualified to Be a KTC?"

1. Can you relate to the four common fears of being a KTC discussed in this chapter? If so, which ones? Why?

2. Make a list of your gifts and abilities. Ask someone who loves you to identify what he or she sees as your strengths, and add those to your list.

3. Take a few minutes to write down a private list of changes that you know God wants to make in your life. Write a prayer of willingness, committing to make those changes for Him.

4. Do you know some good professional Christian counselors in your area? Share their names and phone numbers.

5. How do you think a KTC could help someone who is also receiving professional counseling?

6. Why do you think this statement is true: "As you cultivate and keep your excitement about God, His work will be fresh in your heart—and you will be a delight to others." How do you keep excitement and His work fresh in your heart?

Chapter 3: Getting a Handle on the Big Picture

1. Write about a problem you have recently encountered either personally or as a KTC. What Bible verses would you use to deal with someone in that situation and why?

2. What could God do in the situation you described above, if He worked according to your faith?

3. Share an impossible thing (miracle) that God has done, whether in your life or in somebody else's.

4. What does it mean to "lance the boil" when someone comes with a problem?

5. How do you build your own trust in God before communicating about trusting God to others?

6. Make a note of the Scriptures you would use if someone were to ask
you if God can help hurting women.

Chapter 4: The Bottom Line of Most Problems

1. The unforgiving servant forgot what it was like to be forgiven. Make
a private list of the things you have been forgiven of by God. Write
a prayer of thanksgiving for God's forgiveness without mentioning
your sin. Share your prayer.
2. Is God speaking to you about something or someone you need to
forgive right now? Walk yourself through the steps to forgiveness.
3. From your experience, what are some of the "torturers" that hound
those with unforgiveness in their hearts?
4. When you are hurt, why do you think it is important to acknowledge and recognize the pain as well as the incident?
5. Without naming a specific issue, discuss how long it took you to
heal emotionally after you forgave with your will.

Chapter 5: When the Heartache Seems Unexplainable

1. Read 1 Corinthians 10:13. How can this be applied to troubles? Are
there temptations in trouble? What are yours?
2. What would cause a woman to step out from behind the hedge of
God's protection? How does she get back in the hedge?
3. Has there been an unexplainable tragedy in your life? Where are you
in the process of dealing with it before God?
4. In Revelation 3:19 God says, "Those whom I love, I reprove and
discipline." Discuss the different ways He does this and why.
5. We think that "good" is when everything is going well. What is it
that God calls good?
6. If we offer the sacrifice of thanksgiving, does that mean we have
to be grateful or glad about our pain and heartache? What does it
mean to say thank You to God for things we don't like?

Chapter 6: Keeping Your Priorities Straight

1. List the God-given priorities in Matthew 22:37, Titus 2:3-5, 1 Timothy 5:4, and Galatians 6:10. Keeping priorities is a biblical principle. How would the priorities you have listed translate to a single woman's life?
2. In what areas do you struggle with your priorities?
3. Is your personality overly compassionate, or do you seem to lack compassion?
4. How does this affect your ministry with regard to setting proper boundaries, protecting your home, time, and so forth.
5. How are you rejuvenated and restored?

Chapter 7: Moving On to Spiritual Maturity

1. Do the "Falling in Love with Jesus" project (page 87).
2. Share what you have learned through the study and what difference the new insights have made in your life.

SUGGESTIONS FOR FURTHER STUDY

1. Go through part 2 of this book and do each project for yourself.
2. After each project, answer the following questions:
   a. What did you learn about yourself through the project?
   b. Why would this project be beneficial for someone in that situation?
   c. Did other projects come to mind as you worked on this one? If so, share them.

for leaders

TRAINING OTHERS TO BECOME KITCHEN TABLE COUNSELORS

Though this book is for individual women who want to better understand how they can help hurting women, it can also be used as a resource and manual for church leaders who want to train groups of women to become Kitchen Table Counselors. Here are my recommendations for how to use this book in a group setting.

1. *Plan to meet weekly* for eight weeks.

2. *Make it a closed group.* Only include women who are already working in some capacity with other women, for instance as a small-group leader, Sunday school teacher, mentor, and so forth. Create a separate group for those who have no experience. The inexperienced women will drive the discussion in a different direction, making it less profitable for women who are already doing a form of Kitchen Table Counseling.

3. *Limit the class size* to no more than fifteen, so that everyone can participate easily in the discussions. (If you have women you can appoint

to lead discussion groups, you can have a larger class size.).

4. Each person needs to *commit to attending* every session and to doing the weekly homework, which includes reading a chapter from this book and answering the corresponding questions. The homework should take between one and two hours to complete.

5. *Lay ground rules for confidentiality* for this group and every KTC interaction. First, everyone must commit not to share details that come out in class with others outside the group. Second, individual stories shared within the group should be discussed only in the group setting. (This is so that someone else's problem is not discussed without them being present and to avoid any suggestion of gossip.) Third, be sure to maintain confidentiality when discussing examples of counseling sessions, ensuring the complete anonymity of the parties involved.

6. *Set a time.* Each session should be a minimum of one and a half hours, with thirty minutes of discussing and clarifying the principles in the chapter. During that time, share from your experience. Plan a full hour for discussion of the questions. The number and personality of women in the group could make it necessary for a longer class time or a very directive style on the part of the leader. Everyone should have the opportunity to share her insights so the group is not dominated by a vocal few.

7. *Request that each woman read the chapter* to be discussed and do the questions before the meeting.

WEEK 1

During the first thirty minutes

Summarize what you feel are the key points in chapter 1 and share your spiritual journey.

Refer the group to the Topical Scriptural Reference Index in the back of the book so they can get an idea of the variety of topics and the verses that address them. It is important to emphasize the Word of God and the need for the KTC to spend time studying it. Remember that in John 8:31-32 Jesus says, "If you *hold to my teaching,* . . . *then* you will know the truth, and the truth will set you free" (NIV, emphasis mine). To help our counselees know the truth, the KTC must know the Word.

During the discussion period

Go through the discussion questions for chapter 1 in "For the KTC in Training," seeking to facilitate everyone's interaction and sharing. Ask each person to pinpoint problems or situations that they need to work through. Offer to meet privately with anyone who needs to resolve issues she has identified in her life. A KTC does not have to be perfect; she can be used of God to help others as long as she is following God's guidance in her own life. We are all in process.

WEEK 2

During the first thirty minutes

Share your perspective on what makes an effective KTC.

Discuss why and when to send someone to a medical doctor and/or a professional counselor. Help the group understand the role they can play as KTCs with someone who is undergoing professional counseling or medical treatment.

If you have time, consider taking a passage of Scripture and showing how you would use it to help encourage or work with someone struggling with a particular problem.

During the discussion period

Go through the questions for chapter 2 in "For the KTC in Training." Be conscious of the fact that some things may be hard for a woman to talk about in a large group. If you find this to be true for someone, suggest that she find a trusted confidant for sharing later some of the more private things she has identified.

WEEK 3

During the first thirty minutes

Briefly review the foundational principles from chapter 3, being sure to answer any questions that come up. Point out that these principles are guidelines and that they do not all apply to every counseling situation. If time allows, tell the group about a counseling situation in which you applied some of these principles.

Walk the KTCs through the list of things to do in a first counseling session, and expand on the reasons for those things.

During the discussion period

The discussion questions for chapter 3 are designed to remind the KTC of what God is able to do through His Word and His people. Talk about them with the group and give the group members plenty of time to share. Encourage the women to take notes from the answers of the others.

WEEK 4

During the first thirty minutes

Forgiveness is foundational in the Christian walk and an important part of Kitchen Table Counseling. Many people have problems understanding what forgiveness is and is not, so be sure to ask the group about their response to the key points in this chapter. Review what forgiveness is not as well as the steps to forgiveness. Point out that we can't help someone else forgive if we haven't gone through the process ourselves. Share your perspective on this with the group.

During the discussion period

When discussing the questions, make sure that the emphasis is not placed on people's sin, but on what God does with it. Be careful to facilitate the conversation so that what is talked about is uplifting for those who hear.

WEEK 5

During the first thirty minutes

This may be a difficult chapter for you to teach. However, every KTC needs to have an understanding of the sovereignty of God and to be able to help others look past their circumstances and see His direction. Review the key points from chapter 5 and ask the group for any questions they have about what they have read.

Probably one of the most difficult principles to accept and teach is to thank God *for* the heartache. You will need to spend time on this point. Remember that it is a sacrifice of thanksgiving that expresses trust in God, regardless of what we feel about it. Both Hilda's and Carol King's story underline that truth.

During the discussion period

Go through the questions and have the group members share their answers. There may be tears and unanswerable questions. Emphasize God's love for each person even in the face of the whys.

WEEK 6

During the first thirty minutes

This chapter is meant to help the KTC maintain balance in her life. Making and maintaining boundaries is an important part of helping others.

Talk about ways women in the group can turn the pain and poison they hear over to God and not carry it home to the family.

Expand on ways to help the KTC restore her spirit. Make suggestions for spending time with God and feeding the soul. To help ease the potential guilt they may feel about taking care of themselves, talk about how Jesus did that.

During the discussion period

As you take the group through the questions in "For the KTC in Training," seek to make each woman feel safe enough to share her priorities and her struggles in maintaining them. Those already involved in Kitchen Table Counseling will probably want to talk about the challenges they face. They can encourage each other by sharing the things they have learned and the difficulties they have encountered.

Continue to emphasize the need for confidentiality.

WEEK 7

During the first thirty minutes

Chapter 7 deals with moving from crisis counseling to a mentoring relationship. Help the group see the importance and value of building into a person's life long-term.

Read 1 Corinthians 4:14-21 and discuss the biblical pattern for mentoring laid out there.

During the discussion period

The questions for this week are designed for personal reflection. Encourage the group to look back on the past weeks of study and share what they have learned and what difference it has made in their lives.

Assign each woman one of the topics in part 2 of the book for next week. Have each read the chapter, be prepared to review it for those who did not read it, and share what she learned. Ask each to answer the questions in the "For the KTC in Training" with regard to the topic assigned to her.

WEEK 8

For this final week, spend time allowing each woman to review the topic section she read. Have her give her insights and share what she might do or has done in a similar case.

At the end of your time together, spend time praying for one another. Have each woman pray for the person on her left (or right), thanking God for her gifts and abilities and for what she has contributed to the group. Finally, ask for God's special blessing on her life and her ministry.

topical scripture reference index

Feel free to make a copy of this list and place it at the back of your Bible for easy reference when counseling others.

1 Thessalonians 5:11-15
Revelation 7:17

Complaining
Lamentations 3:39-40

Confronting
1 Samuel 24:8-12
Matthew 5:23-24; 18:15
2 Corinthians 2:4
Galatians 6:1

Courage
Joshua 1:5-6,8-9
1 Samuel 17:45
1 Chronicles 28:9-10
Psalm 27:13-14
Isaiah 50:4-5
Haggai 2:4

Dating
1 Corinthians 7:1-2
2 Corinthians 6:14-16

Death
Deuteronomy 32:39
Job 12:9-10
Ecclesiastes 3:2
Isaiah 25:8
Acts 17:24-26

Death to Self and Sin
Romans 6:11-13
1 Corinthians 15:31
Galatians 2:20
Philippians 2:5-8; 3:10-13

Debt
Romans 13:8

Deliverance
Exodus 14:13-15
2 Kings 6:11-23
Isaiah 61:1-3
Jeremiah 1:17-19

Zechariah 4:6
Matthew 18:18
John 8:36
Romans 16:20

Depression
Psalm 143:7-9
Isaiah 58:10-11
Jeremiah 8:18-22
Ezekiel 34:11-12
Hosea 6:1-3
Micah 7:7-8

Discipleship
Matthew 10:32-40
Luke 6:40; 14:33
Acts 14:22

Disciple, How to
1 Corinthians 4:14-21

Discipline
Revelation 3:19

Discouragement
Psalm 73
Isaiah 51:12

Disobedience
Joshua 23:12-13
Psalm 78:8-10
Jeremiah 9:12-14

Do Not Rebuke Elders
1 Timothy 5:1-2

Fairness
Genesis 18:25
Ezekiel 20:43-44

Faith
Genesis 15:6; 18:14
1 Chronicles 29:11-13
Habakkuk 2:4
Matthew 13:58; 19:26

Mark 2:5; 9:24
Hebrews 11
1 John 5:4-5

Faithfulness
Daniel 3:16-18
2 Timothy 2:13
James 1:12

Fear
Genesis 3:10; 21:17
Deuteronomy 1:21; 3:22; 31:6
2 Chronicles 20:3
Psalms 112:7; 118:5-6
Isaiah 41:10; 43:1-3; 44:8
Luke 12:32
2 Timothy 1:7

Forbidden Things
Jeremiah 2:13; 45:5
1 Corinthians 6:12

Forsaken Wife
Isaiah 54:4-6

God's Blessing
Deuteronomy 23:14; 28:1-6;
    30:19-20
Psalms 65:4; 84:1-12; 92:12-15
Isaiah 64:3-5
Jeremiah 31:10-14
Mark 10:29-30

God's Encouragement
1 Kings 19:1-21
2 Kings 6:17
Isaiah 40:28-31; 54:11-13; 66:13
Lamentations 3:21-26,32-33
Zechariah 4:6
Mark 10:27
Ephesians 2:14
Philippians 1:6

God's Forgiveness
Nehemiah 9:17

Psalms 32:5; 103:3-4,12
Isaiah 43:25; 44:22-23; 55:7-8
Luke 7:47

God's Goodness
Genesis 50:19-20
Psalms 73:28; 78:10-29; 86:5
Isaiah 30:18-21; 49:15-16; 53:4-5
Ezekiel 34:26
Hosea 10:12
Nahum 1:7
Romans 2:4; 9:33

God Hates These Things
Proverbs 6:16-19

God's Leading
Acts 8:26-40; 23:11

God's Love
Genesis 35:3; 39:21
Psalms 52:8; 136:1-26
Proverbs 3:12
Isaiah 40:11; 49:15-16; 54:10
Jeremiah 31:3-5
Hosea 14:4
Micah 7:18-19
Matthew 10:29-31
Romans 8:35-39

God's Mercy and Grace
Psalms 78:35-39; 84:11-12;
    94:17-19
Isaiah 1:18; 42:3
Jeremiah 9:24
Ezekiel 34:26
Malachi 3:16
Matthew 20:1-14
2 Corinthians 9:8; 12:9

God's Power for Us
Ephesians 1:18-23

God's Presence
Genesis 28:16-17

Psalms 16:8-9; 31:20
Isaiah 43:1-3; 58:2
Jeremiah 23:23-24
Ezekiel 44:28
Zephaniah 3:17

God's Protection
Genesis 19:29
Deuteronomy 31:8
Ezra 8:21-31
Job 1:10
Psalms 34:7; 125:2; 146:9
Colossians 3:3
James 4:7-8

God's Provision
Psalm 81:13-16
Matthew 6:25-34; 10:29-31
Romans 8:32
Philippians 4:19

God's Purpose
Romans 8:28-29

God's Strength and Support
2 Chronicles 16:9; 20:20-22
Psalms 7:11; 16:5-6; 18:16-19;
   62:8; 71:5
Isaiah 52:12
Zechariah 10:12
Ephesians 2:14
Colossians 1:9-11
2 Timothy 4:17

God's Will
Psalms 25:14-15; 32:8; 36:9;
   119:130
Proverbs 3:5-6; 16:9
Isaiah 52:12
Jeremiah 29:11-13
John 7:17; 10:27
Romans 12:2
1 Corinthians 1:7
Philippians 3:14-15

Gossip
Proverbs 26:20
Romans 2:1
1 Corinthians 4:5
James 2:12-13

Hasty Decisions
Proverbs 19:2

Heart, The
Psalm 51:17
Proverbs 4:23
Jeremiah 11:20; 17:9-10
Ezekiel 6:9; 11:19-20; 18:31;
   36:26-27
Matthew 12:34; 15:8; 22:37-39
Mark 6:52
Luke 24:32
1 Thessalonians 2:4

Holy Spirit
Romans 8:9
1 Corinthians 2:12; 3:16

Hope for the Lost
Isaiah 42:16
Jeremiah 24:6-7

Immorality
Genesis 39:9
Proverbs 9:17-18; 11:22
Matthew 5:27-28; 19:9
1 Corinthians 6:17-20
1 Thessalonians 4:3-8

Jealousy
James 3:16

Joy
Nehemiah 8:10
Psalm 16:11; 45:7; 87:7; 92:4;
   119:111
Jeremiah 15:16; 31:12
Zephaniah 3:17

John 15:11
Jude 24

Judgment for Believer
2 Corinthians 5:10
James 5:9
1 Peter 4:17-19

Loss of Blessing
1 Chronicles 13:6-14
Psalm 106:15
Jeremiah 4:18
Ezekiel 33:17-18
Hosea 4:9-10

Marriage
Genesis 2:24
Romans 15:5-6
Hebrews 13:4

Mature Women Teach
Titus 2:3-5

Ministry
1 Chronicles 28:20
Ezra 7:10
Psalm 78:70-72
Isaiah 42:16
Jeremiah 3:15; 10:21
Daniel 12:3
Haggai 2:4
Malachi 2:6-7
Matthew 20:25-28
John 14:12
Romans 12:15
1 Corinthians 2:2-4
1 Thessalonians 2:7-8
2 Timothy 2:24-25

Missions
Psalms 2:8; 96:3-4
Isaiah 42:5-9; 49:6; 55:12-13
Habakkuk 2:14
Matthew 24:14
Mark 16:15

Acts 1:8
Romans 10:14-15
2 John 6-8

Obedience
Daniel 11:32
Luke 5:4-5

Our Forgiveness
Matthew 6:15; 18:21-25
Mark 11:25
2 Corinthians 2:6-8

Parents
Exodus 20:12
Psalm 27:10; 68:5

Peace
Ephesians 2:14
Philippians 4:4-9

Physical weakness
2 Corinthians 4:7-10

Prayer
Genesis 24:12-14
Joshua 10:14
1 Chronicles 4:10
2 Chronicles 20:6-12; 33:12-13; 34:27
Psalms 4:4; 66:19-20; 91:14-16; 116:1; 138:3; 141:1-3
Proverbs 15:8
Isaiah 55:6
Lamentations 2:19
Ezekiel 22:29-31
Daniel 6:10; 9:3-19; 10:12-13
Matthew 7:7-11; 18:19-20; 21:21-22
Luke 18:35-43; 21:34-36
John 15:7
Acts 10:4
Romans 8:26-27
Colossians 4:2-3
Hebrews 7:25

James 4:2
1 John 5:14
Revelation 5:8; 8:3-4

Pride
Isaiah 2:11-12; 3:16
Hosea 13:6
Obadiah 3-4

Priorities
Galatians 6:10

Rape and Molestation
Mark 7:14-23

Rebellion
Psalm 32:9
Isaiah 3:8-9; 17:10-11; 63:7-10
Jeremiah 2:5,20,35; 3:22; 5:3,22-25;
    7:23-24
Ezekiel 2:8

Relationships
Romans 12:18
1 Corinthians 5:9-11
2 Corinthians 3:17
Ephesians 4:15,25-32
Colossians 3:8-16
1 Timothy 5:1-4

Repentance and Restoration
Deuteronomy 30:2-6,11-18
Ezra 9:1-15
Psalms 51:10-12; 139:23-24
Isaiah 61:1-7
Jeremiah 3:12-13,22; 4:3-4;
    31:17-20
Ezekiel 18:21-22,30-32
Romans 2:4
2 Peter 3:9
Revelation 3:19

Resistance to God's Work
Ezra 4:1-24
Psalm 109:2-5

Isaiah 54:17

Sacrifice
2 Samuel 24:24
Psalm 50:9-15

Salvation
John 1:12
Romans 10:9,13
Ephesians 2:8-9
1 John 1:9
Revelation 3:20; 22:16-17

Satan
Lamentations 1:9
Zechariah 3:1-7
Mark 9:29
Luke 10:17-20
John 19:11
2 Corinthians 4:4
James 4:7-8
1 Peter 5:8-9

Self-Image
Exodus 3:11; 4:10-11; 19:4-5
Psalm 139:13-16
Jeremiah 1:5
Romans 12:3-4
1 Corinthians 3:16-17
2 Corinthians 3:5
Ephesians 1:3-14
Philippians 4:13

Sexual Abstinence
Matthew 4:1-11
Ephesians 5:3
1 Thessalonians 4:3-8

Sexual Purity
1 Corinthians 7:1-2
Ephesians 5:11-12

Sickness and Healing
Psalm 71:5-6,9
Matthew 12:28

notes

chapter 2

1. Oswald Chambers, *My Utmost for His Highest* (Grand Rapids, MI: Discovery House, 1992), June 19 reading.

chapter 4

1. *"Reader's Digest" Family Word Finder: A New Thesaurus of Synonyms and Antonyms in Dictionary Form*, ed. The Reader's Digest in association with Stuart B. Flexner (Pleasantville, NY: Reader's Digest Association Inc., 1975), 321.
2. Dan B. Allender and Tremper Longman III, *Bold Love* (Colorado Springs, CO: NavPress, 1992), 16.
3. Our thanks to Verna Birkey for this illustration.
4. Judy Wortley, *Forgiving the Murderer of My Child* (Clovis, CA: Training with Vision, 2002), 79–84. Reprinted with permission.

chapter 6

1. CBS Broadcasting Inc., *The Early Show*, New York, December 2, 2003.

chapter 9

1. From www.pureintimacy.org/gr/intimacy/understanding/a0000128 .cfm.
2. From www.pureintimacy.org/gr/intimacy/understanding/a0000128 .cfm.
3. From www.pureintimacy.org/gr/intimacy/understanding/a0000128 .cfm.
4. Adapted from Edmund J. Bourne, PhD, *The Anxiety and Phobia Workbook*, 3rd ed. (Oakland, CA: New Harbinger Publications, 2000), 109.

chapter 11

1. Henry Cloud and John Townsend, *Boundaries: When to Say Yes, When to Say No, to Take Control of Your Life* (Grand Rapids, MI: Zondervan, 1992), front dust jacket.
2. Cloud and Townsend, 49.

chapter 12

1. *Random House Webster's College Dictionary* (New York: Random House, 1999), 992.

chapter 15

1. John Gottman, in Malcolm Gladwell, *Blink: The Power of Thinking Without Thinking* (New York: Little, Brown, 2005), 32–33.

chapter 17

1. From www.internet-filter-review.toptenreviews.com/internet -pornography-statistics.html.
2. From www.internet-filter-review.toptenreviews.com/internet -pornography-statistics.html.

chapter 18

1. From www.face2facecounseling.org.
2. From www.athealth.com/Consumer/disorders/SexualAbuse.
3. From www.wickipedia.com.

chapter 20

1. Neil T. Anderson, *The Bondage Breaker: Overcoming Negative Thoughts, Irrational Feelings, and Habitual Sins* (Eugene, OR: Harvest House, 1993), 23.

chapter 21

1. From www.befrienders.org/suicide/statistics.html.
2. From www.sclifeline.org/page3.html.
3. Lynda D. Elliott, *How Can I Help? Caring for People Without Harming Them or Yourself* (Grand Rapids, MI: Chosen Books, 2003), 38.

chapter 22

1. Robert S. McGee, *The Search for Significance: Seeing Your True Worth Through God's Eyes* (Houston: Rapha, 1985), 15.

about the authors

MURIEL L. COOK is a biblical counselor and international conference speaker. She and her husband of fifty-five years, Norman, live in Portland, Oregon. The Cooks have two married daughters and four grandchildren.

SHELLY COOK VOLKHARDT is Muriel's oldest daughter. She is a Bible teacher, conference speaker, and Kitchen Table Counselor. Shelly and her husband, Glen, live in Colorado Springs, Colorado. They have two sons.

For more information about resources and speaking engagements, see www.kitchentablecounseling.com

acknowledgments

A deep thanks to my husband, Norman, who totally believes in me. He is a man of a different spirit who wholly follows the Lord.

Thank you to my dear friends who have cheered me on and prayed for me. My heart is full of love for you.

— MURIEL

With deep love and thanks to many other sister/friends whose love, encouragement, and prayers have sustained me.

Thank you to my precious family — Glen, Culver, Carl, and Genie — for sharing life with me! I love you deeply.

Many thanks to Liz Heaney, whose editing has taught me so much. My thanks and appreciation to all the team at NavPress.

— SHELLY